J940.4
C.1

890

DATE DUE			

RM √ 06/10/09

THE HOLOCAUST

THE HOLOCAUST

BY SEYMOUR ROSSEL

A GROLIER COMPANY

FRANKLIN WATTS
New York/London/Toronto/Sydney
1981

I wish to express my thanks to my family
—Karen, Amy, and Deborah—
who understood my many nights of vigil
and were patient and loving throughout.

Seymour Rossel
Chappaqua, New York
March, 1981

Maps courtesy of Vantage Art, Inc.

Library of Congress Cataloging in Publication Data

Rossel, Seymour.
The Holocaust.

Bibliography: p.
Includes index.
Summary: Discusses how, between 1938 and 1945,
the Nazis planned and carried out a program of
extermination against the Jews of Europe now
known as the Holocaust, and how the Holocaust
continues to affect our everyday lives.
1. Holocaust, Jewish (1939-1945)—
Juvenile literature.
[1. Holocaust, Jewish (1939-1945)]
I. Title.
D810.J4R665   940.53'15'03924   81-10515
ISBN 0-531-04351-7   AACR2

CONTENTS

*Dedicated to those of my family
I never had the opportunity of knowing,
whose unknown graves I will never
have the privilege of visiting,
whose lives would have made mine richer;
and to my uncle
who perished in the struggle to
end the senseless slaughter.*
S.R.

THE HOLOCAUST

HITLER'S EUROPE, 1941

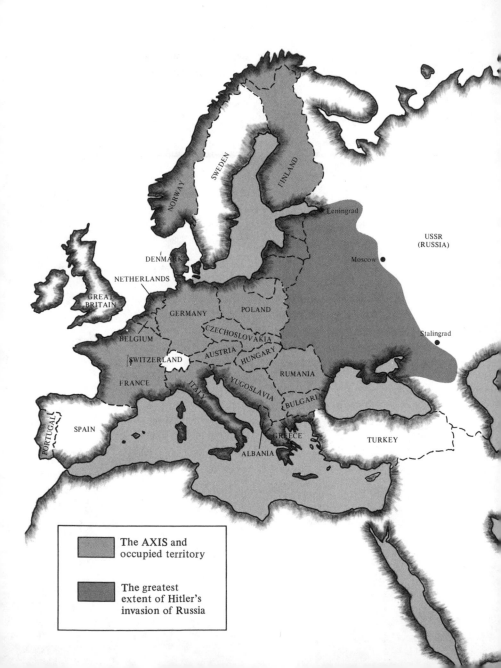

NORWAY
SWEDEN
FINLAND
Leningrad
USSR (RUSSIA)
DENMARK
Moscow
NETHERLANDS
GREAT BRITAIN
GERMANY
POLAND
CZECHOSLOVAKIA
Stalingrad
BELGIUM
AUSTRIA
HUNGARY
SWITZERLAND
FRANCE
ITALY
YUGOSLAVIA
RUMANIA
BULGARIA
PORTUGAL
SPAIN
GREECE
TURKEY
ALBANIA

The AXIS and occupied territory

The greatest extent of Hitler's invasion of Russia

INTRODUCTION: THE HOLOCAUST AND ITS MEANING

Nearly six million Jews were killed in what historians have called the Holocaust. A holocaust is a conflagration, a great raging fire consuming in its path all that lives. Just such a murderous fire burned for a few short years during World War II in Germany and in the countries that Germany invaded and conquered. When this Holocaust was over, nearly one-third of all the Jews in the world had been put to death.

They were not just the victims of war, though World War II was being fought. They were not just victims of neglect, although many died of exposure, disease, and starvation. They were not just victims of politics, although some were put to death for openly disagreeing with the government. They were not just victims of senseless mobs, although Nazi officials encouraged anti-Jewish rioting. The Jews of Europe who died in the Holocaust were the victims of a careful, well-organized plan.

This plan had one purpose: to destroy the Jews. The Nazis who designed the program called it "the

Final Solution to the Jewish Question." Six million people were murdered because they were born of Jewish parents, had one Jewish parent, or had at least one Jewish grandparent.

Of course, people have been killing one another since the beginning of history. And in our times—through newspapers, magazines, radio, and television—murder has become a part of everyday life. Twenty years ago millions watched as the man accused of shooting President John F. Kennedy was himself shot to death in front of a television camera. Over the next ten years television brought us images of soldiers killing and being killed in a war thousands of miles away. Just to open the daily newspaper is to discover a world that seems full of violence. Why should anyone read about a crime that happened forty years ago?

Why read about the Holocaust?

Extermination as Official Policy. What sets the Holocaust starkly apart from the violent crimes which tend to fill our daily news reports is the appalling fact that the murder of innocent civilians was a government policy. There have been, and are, other examples of government policy intended to subjugate, even to exterminate, a group of people. But never in history has such a policy been carried out on such a scale.

The Weight of Numbers: the Holocaust Balance Sheet. The sheer size of the catastrophe also gives the Holocaust lasting significance. A few individuals—the Nazis—within just a few years set about to accomplish mass murder in the firm belief that no one would even attempt to stop them.

AN ESTIMATE OF
JEWISH VICTIMS
OF THE HOLOCAUST

4,565,000	Polish and Russian Jews
125,000	German Jews
65,000	Austrian Jews
277,000	Czechoslovakian Jews
402,000	Hungarian Jews
83,000	French Jews
24,000	Belgian Jews
700	Jews of Luxembourg
7,500	Italian Jews
106,000	Jews of the Netherlands
760	Norwegian Jews
40,000	Rumanian Jews
60,000	Yugoslavian Jews
65,000	Greek Jews
5,820,960	TOTAL LOSS

[Source: *Encyclopaedia Judaica*]

It is impossible to know exactly how many Jews were put to death. At the time, the Nazis kept careful lists, many of which were stored in one central office. But they set fire to these files so they would not be captured by the advancing Allies. Nevertheless, other records were captured at the end of the war. On the basis of these, although they are not complete, it is estimated that between 5,200,000 and 6,000,000 Jews were put to death or died in the Holocaust. The loss of so many was in itself a catastrophe. In fact it was the largest loss of human life ever suffered by any one people.

Jews were not the only victims of the Holocaust. Many Gypsies were destroyed. The Nazis said that the Gypsies were racially inferior and deserved to die. Slavs were murdered for the same reason. The mentally retarded, the insane, and the physically deformed were also put to death. Those said to be enemies of the German nation (including many who spoke out against Hitler) were killed as well.

The Human Element. Numbers alone cannot tell the story. After all, we are speaking of human beings—people who had families, worked, walked in parks, went to the movies, visited museums; people who listened to music, who danced and sang, who studied and played games, who ate in restaurants, and who gave parties. Each was a unique human being with special hopes, wishes, feelings, and needs; with parents, friends, and relatives.

Understanding the Past. Another major reason for careful study of the Holocaust is our need to understand the past. Like fire marshals sifting the ashes once the flames have been extinguished, scholars are seeking to discover the causes of this human tragedy. How did such a great outpouring of hatred come about? How did it come to be government policy? Were there warning signs of what was about to take place—signs that no one read at the time, but that we may discover now?

The philosopher George Santayana wrote that we must learn from history, for "those who cannot remember the past are condemned to repeat it." Scholars who study the Holocaust would like to ensure that nothing like it can happen again.

Discovering Responsibility. In 1960 Adolf Eichmann, the German who had been most directly responsible for carrying out the policy of the "Final Solution," was put on trial and hanged for "crimes against the Jewish people and against humanity." The trial of Eichmann shed new light on questions of political and moral responsibility.

The crime of the Holocaust was so great that there was a natural human reluctance to look into it too deeply. Before World War II, people could still believe that the world was slowly but surely becoming a better place. New technology was making life easier and more comfortable. Western Europeans and Americans regarded their way of life as the most forward-looking, the most civilized in the world. Germans, Frenchmen, and Britons were teaching the so-called backward peoples of Asia and Africa what true civilization meant.

Suddenly a civilized European nation, Germany, began to ignore all the rules of this civilization. Germany made treaties and broke them without warning

[5]

or apology. The German government began to imprison leading scholars, scientists, and public figures just for protesting against government policies. Germany started the most destructive war in history. Nazi troops and officials seized German Jews and Jews from the conquered countries, and sent them to forced labor and death. The German government did all these things, and the German people were silent.

The modern German nation had fallen below the confident standards of the so-called civilized world. It was suddenly necessary to face the discouraging fact that no nation is so civilized as to have no potential for evil. Moreover, a nation is nothing more than a collection of individuals. No matter what a group, an army, or a government may do, decisions are made and actions are taken by individuals who then bear the responsibility for them. After World War II, this, above all, was recognized as the message of the Holocaust.

No man is an island, entire of itself;
every man is a piece of the continent,
a part of the main;
if a clod be washed away by the sea,
Europe is the less,
as well as if a promontory were,
as well as if a manor of thy friend's
or of thine own were;
any man's death diminishes me,
because I am involved in mankind;
and therefore never send to know
for whom the bell tolls;
it tolls for thee.

John Donne
Devotions XVII, 1623

1
HITLER'S RISE TO POWER

World War I ended in disaster for the German nation. In the aftermath of the war, poverty-stricken Germans continued to die of starvation and disease. The nation's wealth had been spent in fighting the Allies. The Treaty of Versailles reduced the area of the German Empire by one tenth. Germany was made to admit that it was guilty of starting the war. The German government was forbidden to raise an army of more than a hundred thousand men, or to build any large weapons of war. Most damaging of all, the treaty stipulated that Germany pay the Allies enormous amounts of money as reparations, to compensate for the suffering caused by the war. The already impoverished citizens were forced to pay heavy taxes to make up these reparation payments.

Not only the economy, but the spirit of the country was destroyed by the Versailles Treaty of 1919. Of the nations of Europe, Germany above all had taken pride in its military strength, and now its armies were reduced. The new government was weak and many small parties sprang up to oppose it. Family unity shattered as young people lost respect for their parents and began to rebel against them. In short, Germany's faith in itself was shaken deeply by defeat.

The Search for a Scapegoat. Even before Adolf Hitler and his political party rose to power, Germany was a nation in search of some person or group on whom to lay the blame for defeat. The Jews were singled out. They were the largest German minority —an easy target for prejudice.

Germany had a long history of anti-Semitism, religious prejudice against Jews. As far back as 1542 the great German Protestant leader Martin Luther had written a booklet called *Against the Jews and Their Lies.* Even earlier the Catholic Church had taught that the Jews had killed Christ and should therefore be hated. As the twentieth century dawned, many Germans had come to identify themselves as members of the "Aryan race," which they considered superior to any other group of people in the world. Yet the Jews continued to call themselves the "chosen people," as they were called in the Bible. To some, this alone may have made the Germans and the Jews seem natural enemies in conflict over who was superior. In 1890 Hermann Ahlwardt, a member of the German parliament, wrote an essay called "The War of Desperation between the Aryan People and Judaism." He called for the extermination of the Jews.

Just before World War I there was a short period of patriotism shared by all, Jew and non-Jew alike. All Germans took pride in the fatherland. During World War I Jews served along with non-Jews, fighting and dying in the armies of Germany. But when the war ended in defeat the German people, searching for someone to blame, looked back to those they had hated in the past, the Jews.

Hitler Enters German Politics. In 1919 in the city of Munich, Hitler joined a group called the German Workers' Party. He became one of seven committee members who headed the party. This group held meetings to discuss the present government and its weakness, to remember the better days before World War I, to talk about the danger to Germany of the Bolsheviks (Communists) who had recently come to power in Russia, and to discuss the danger within Germany—the Jews.

Hitler wanted more than just to sit and discuss ideas. He wanted to create a force for change. For this purpose he needed many followers. But he was unsure of himself. Could he lead others? Could he make others listen to his ideas and follow him? He was prepared to try. He planned an evening of speeches, and wrote out invitations by hand asking people to attend one of the party's meetings. The committee members came—and no one else.

But Hitler was determined. Planning another evening, he sent out mimeographed invitations. Now eleven people came. At last Hitler decided to use anti-Semitism as a tool. With the last funds of the club, Hitler placed an advertisement in a local anti-Semitic newspaper, promising an evening of anti-Semitic speeches. This time he attracted a crowd. John Toland, in his biography of Hitler, tells what happened on that fateful night:

. . . by 7 p.m. seventy people had collected in the smoky room. There is no record of the reception given the main speaker but almost from the moment Adolf Hitler stepped behind the crude lectern placed atop the head table the audience was "electrified." He was supposed to speak for twenty minutes, but went on for half an hour, spilling out a stream of denunciations, threats and promises. . . . by the time he sat down to loud applause sweat covered his face. He was exhausted but elated "and what before I had simply felt deep down in my heart, without being able to put it to the test [Hitler wrote], proved to be true; I could speak!" [John Toland, *Adolf Hitler*]

That evening Hitler discovered his two most powerful weapons: the appeal of anti-Semitism and his own ability to speak and excite people. From then on the meetings began to grow in numbers and so did the German Workers' Party.

Organizing the Party. Hitler set about organizing his new political party. In 1920 it was renamed the National Socialist German Workers' Party—the Nazi party for short. In 1928 the party won eight hundred thousand votes. Even then it was more than just a political group. Hitler had already begun turning it into a kind of military operation. He trained "storm troopers" to act as militia. And many leaders who remembered past German military might began to support the Nazi party and its troops.

With these former army leaders on his side, Hitler felt the time had come for direct action. On November 8, 1923, he and his storm troopers surrounded a group of government officials in a beer hall in Munich. Hitler told them that he wanted to turn the government over to the military. He forced them to swear loyalty to his "revolution." But when the officials were freed, they had Hitler arrested. He was tried and sent to prison with a five-year sentence. His "beer hall *Putsch*" had failed, but news of it spread and Hitler's name was heard far and wide for the first time.

Hitler's Ideas. Hitler served only nine months of his prison term; then he was set free by the authorities, many of whom were sympathetic to his cause. While he was in prison, Hitler organized his ideas into a book. He dictated the book to his prison mate, Rudolf Hess. The book was called *Mein Kampf* (My Struggle) and it became the Nazi bible.

Like most extremists Hitler was filled with prejudices. And the greatest prejudice of all he saved for the Jewish people. From the beginning of his book to the end, Hitler spoke of the Jewish people as the cause of the troubles and ills that Germany was suffering:

> If we pass all the causes of the German collapse in review, the ultimate and most decisive remains the failure to recognize the racial problem and especially the Jewish menace. [Adolf Hitler, *Mein Kampf*]

Hitler believed that the Jews were natural enemies of the "superior" Aryan race (to which the Germans belonged). It was, he felt, unnatural for Jews and Aryans to intermarry and have children:

> Any crossing of two beings not at exactly the same level produces a medium. . . . Such mating is contrary to the will of Nature . . . [Adolf Hitler, *Mein Kampf*]

Hitler argued that the Jews were dangerous because, in his view, they controlled the German nation. He believed that they controlled not only money and land, but the press as well. And the Jews, he said, were using the press to tell people what to think:

> With all his perseverance and dexterity [the Jew] seizes possession of [the press]. With it he slowly begins to grip and ensnare, to guide and to push all public life, since he is in a position to create and direct that power which, under the name of "public opinion," is better known today than a few decades ago. [Adolf Hitler, *Mein Kampf*]

But for Hitler the greatest danger was what he called the danger of the "blood." He was afraid that Jewish blood would poison the pure blood of the Aryan Germans:

> [The Jew] poisons the blood of others, but preserves his own. The Jew almost never marries a Christian woman; it is the Christian who marries a Jewess. The [children] however, take after the Jewish side. . . . In order to mask his activity and lull his victims . . .

[the Jew] talks more and more of the equality of all men without regard to race and color. The fools begin to believe him. [Adolf Hitler, *Mein Kampf*]

And what did Hitler think was the goal of the Jews? What did they wish to accomplish?

[The Jew's] ultimate goal in this stage is the victory of "democracy," or, as he understands it: the rule of parliamentarianism. [Adolf Hitler, *Mein Kampf*]

Hitler's Power Grows. Freed from prison, Hitler turned back to the work of building and expanding his party and its troopers. In the elections of 1930 the Nazi party won six and a half million votes. They had become the second largest political party in Germany, and where before they had held only twelve seats in the Reichstag, now they held more than a hundred. Why had a small unknown political party from Austria suddenly become the second most powerful in Germany?

The Great Depression. In the fall of 1929 a shock wave began in the city of New York which was destined to help bring Hitler to power in far-off Germany. The Wall Street stock market crashed. The trading of stocks came to an abrupt halt when the value of the stocks suddenly fell to practically nothing. Millionaires became paupers overnight. The middle class saw its savings and investments disappear. People who had invested in stocks and bonds suddenly had nothing left. Banks failed and companies went bankrupt;

people who had placed their money in savings accounts and checking accounts found that they could not draw their money out because the banks had been shut down. Factories and stores closed. Jobs were scarce.

Germany's economy after World War I had been built on foreign loans, especially loans from the United States, and on world trade, which was also based on a system of loans and notes of credit. As a result, the fate of Germany (and of other countries as well) was tied up with that of the United States. When world trade and commerce collapsed, the German economy collapsed with it. Now millions of Germans were out of work. The middle class saw its savings and investments disappear. To pay their debts, people were forced to sell their houses and furnishings. The Depression was the final blow coming on top of Germany's military defeat and the postwar years of inflation and unemployment. In Germany more than in any other country a feeling of utter hopelessness came over the people.

The major political parties were stunned and helpless. Only two parties could turn to the people of Germany to say, "We told you so." One of these was the Communist party, which for years had said that the defeat of capitalism was near. The other was Hitler's party, the Nazis.

Hitler as Speaker. Hitler was tireless. He traveled from city to city by plane, automobile, and railroad. In the final few weeks before the election of 1930, he made as many as three speeches a day. He blamed the loss of the First World War on the old politicians of Germany; he told the people that they had been betrayed by Jewish bankers and moneylenders; he warned those who would listen that the time had come to rebuild Germany's army and prepare for war against the Communists. He promised that there would be jobs for everyone when rebuilding began. Finally, he reminded the people of their lost pride in the fatherland, and he proclaimed the superiority of the Aryan race and German civilization.

In 1919 Hitler had been surprised to discover that he could capture the attention of seventy people. By the mid-1930s he had become a masterful speaker. He spoke at huge rallies organized by the Party, holding thousands of listeners spellbound with his visionary dreams of what Germany could become, and arousing them to a frenzied hatred of Jews, Communists, and political enemies.

1930–1933. In the early 1930s the Depression spread. By 1932 over three million Germans were out of work. The moderate parties were weak and helpless, unable to agree on what to do. More and more the military leaders looked to Hitler for an answer. After all, he was promising to rebuild German military power. More and more the leaders of industry and business looked to Hitler. They saw that new factories and industry would be needed to build up and equip the military forces. More and more the members of the middle class listened to Hitler's promises of new jobs.

Hitler campaigned without stopping, and the Nazi party continued to grow. His storm troopers, called the Brownshirts because of the uniform they wore, grew to an army of about half a million. By 1933 most of the other small anti-Semitic and extreme-right parties had joined forces with the Nazis. And in this moment, when the government needed leadership, the aging president of the German republic, Paul von Hindenburg, was faced with the most difficult decision of his political life. He did not like Hitler. He very much wanted a moderate leader for the German republic. But there was no moderate leader with a real program for helping Germany out of the Depression. And there was no moderate leader who could bring together enough of the votes in the Reichstag to rule the country. Hitler seemed the only possibility.

On January 30, 1933, President von Hindenburg called on Hitler to form a new government and to become the chancellor of Germany. Hitler swore the oath of office, promising to protect the constitution of Germany and its laws, and to be just and fair to all Germans. But even as he spoke these words, he had made plans for a war on democracy.

The Reichstag Fire. New elections had been set for March of 1933, and Hitler wanted to make sure that the Nazis would win these elections decisively. In the second election of 1932 they had lost votes, and had lost some seats in the Reichstag. Hitler was determined to ensure that it would not happen again. Although it is not absolutely certain, most historians believe that Hitler ordered his storm troopers to arrange for a fire in the Reichstag building and to make it seem that the Communists had set the fire.

Even before the fire was set, Hitler and his chief lieutenants drew up lists of enemies to be arrested and accused of the fire. On these lists were many leading members of the Reichstag, leading members of the Communist party inside Germany, and others who had spoken out from time to time against Hitler and against Nazism.

Luck was with Hitler; whether by plan or by accident, his storm troopers discovered a down-and-out Dutchman who happened to be a member of the Communist party. The Dutchman had been heard bragging that the only way to change the government in Germany would be to set fire to government buildings. It is now believed that the Brownshirts set fire to the Reichstag building, using gasoline and other chemicals. It was only a few minutes before the building was ablaze in the night. The Dutchman was immediately arrested; later he was tried and executed.

When Hitler, the new chancellor of Germany, arrived on the scene of the fire, he declared that the burning of the Reichstag was the work of the Communists. With the new elections only a week away, he stepped up his campaign against the "Marxists," the press, and organizations of the political left.

To the old President von Hindenburg the fire came as a great blow. The quick arrest of many of Germany's foremost political leaders left their parties stunned and without direction. The government seemed near collapse. Hitler insisted that the Communists were trying to take over Germany by force, as they had taken over Russia in 1917. Something had to be done, he declared. And he knew just what it should be. He called for von Hindenburg to sign an emergency decree "for the protection of the people and the state."

The decree canceled all individual and civil rights, placing power in the hands of Hitler and his party. It became illegal for Germans to express their opinions freely, or to assemble to hear political speeches or for any other reason. And the decree made it legal for Hitler and his Brownshirts to control what was published in newspapers or broadcast as news over the radio; to open mail, read telegrams, and listen in on telephone conversations; to search houses without warning; to confiscate personal property; and to rule by dictatorship in any of the states of Germany, whenever Hitler thought it necessary.

With von Hindenburg's decree on February 28, 1933, Hitler became Germany's dictator.

2

CONSOLIDATING POWER: ANTI-SEMITISM AS A TOOL

Germany was now a dictatorship. Germans who opposed the Nazis were too frightened to resist. What had frightened them so? For one thing, they thought the Communists were really trying to destroy the government. For another, they were out of work and desperate. And too, they had lost their freedom—even the freedom to protest—and the loss of freedom was frightening in itself. New elections were coming up, but many leaders of the moderate parties had been arrested, and no party except Hitler's was allowed to make political speeches or hold political gatherings.

In spite of all this, most people remained moderate. The Nazis were able to win only 44 percent of the national vote. Hitler was forced to include in his new government some of the moderates of the Social Democratic party. This was only a minor problem for Hitler. For even while he was making his party the legal government of Germany, his Brownshirts looted, wrecked, and burned the offices of the Communist and Socialist parties, arresting and attacking many of their leaders. The Socialist newspaper was banned in many states.

On the day before the newly elected Reichstag met, one of Hitler's key assistants, Heinrich Himmler, announced that the first concentration camp had been set up in a place called Dachau not far from Munich. In this camp, he said, the many arrested Communist and Social Democrat officials could be "concentrated" and held so that they would no longer be a threat to the German republic. A few days later a second concentration camp was set up for the same purpose, and within ten days fifteen thousand persons had been arrested and sent to these two camps.

On July 8, 1933, Hitler declared, "the Party has now become the State." Former political parties were outlawed and it became illegal for any new parties to be formed. By mid-July only the Nazi party remained.

The Nazi "Party." The Communists and the moderate parties had been unable to stop Hitler. They had seen the danger coming, but they were political parties—nothing more. The Nazis were a great deal more:

> In speaking of the Nazi movement as a "party" there is a danger of mistaking its true character. For the Nazi Party was no more a party, in the normal democratic sense of that word, than the Communist Party is today [in Russia]; it was an organized conspiracy against the State. The Party's programme was important to win support. . . . But . . . the real object was to

[22]

get their hands on the State . . . the sole object of the Party was to secure power by one means or another. [Alan Bullock, *Adolf Hitler: A Study in Tyranny*]

To seize control of the state, Hitler had raised his own private army, the *Sturmabteilung,* (SA), commonly known as the Brownshirts. These, especially at first, were often men with criminal backgrounds. Hitler also had his own secret police, the Gestapo, and his own security force, the *Schutzstaffel,* (SS), called the Blackshirts. The SS began as Hitler's bodyguards and became an elite corps in charge of security. Hitler's party was more than a political force; it was also a military presence within Germany.

Using the Law. Still, Hitler's party was not strong enough to take over Germany by force alone. Hitler had discovered that fact many years before in the failure of his "beer hall *Putsch*" in Munich. The Brownshirts could be helpful—as they were in the case of the Reichstag fire and in rounding up those who opposed Hitler after the fire. But Hitler calculated that the best route to real power in Germany was to act within the law. By doing his work legally, Hitler gave the moderates or leftists no excuse for trying to stop him by force. He knew that he could lose everything if the nation's army were called out against him; so he gave no legal reason for that to happen.

The army leaders were pleased. Many of the young officers, and some of the older ones, looked forward to Hitler's rise to power. After all, he had promised to rebuild the army and strengthen it. But more than that, he had made youth movements an important part of his scheme. In the movement called Hitler Youth he and his followers taught the young that Nazism was the hope of the future. Later, when he became the dictator of Germany, he made sure that the same lesson was taught in the public schools, even having textbooks rewritten to say that the Jews were the cause of all Germany's problems, that all Communists were either Jewish or led astray by Jewish ideas, and that only the Nazis could protect Germany. As the young people graduated from Hitler Youth, many found places in the army, and as time went on, the army became more and more supportive of Hitler.

Propaganda. Hitler had become a master of propaganda, the spreading of "official" doctrine—including lies. In his party he even had an official minister of propaganda, a man named Joseph Paul Goebbels.

Just as he used propaganda in the Hitler Youth movement and later in the public schools, Hitler used it to help him convince the people of Germany that he was the answer to their many needs. Once the presidential decree had been signed in 1933, Hitler controlled what was written in newspapers and spoken on the radio (there were no television sets yet). Newspaper reporters and radio announcers soon learned that they would be fired if they disagreed with the government. The newspapers began to print without criticism the "official" propaganda sent out by Goebbels.

Wherever people turned, they heard what Hitler wanted them to hear and read what Hitler wanted them to read. Together, the press and the government taught that the Germans were the greatest race on earth—pure Aryans; this applied especially to large-boned, strong-muscled Germans with blond hair and blue eyes. (Hitler, however, did not fit this description; he was short and dark.) In contrast to the "superior" Aryan race, the Jews were described as "inferior." Last but not least, the Jews, according to Nazi propaganda, were the great enemy—they controlled the banks, the money, the power. It was because of the Jews and their allies, the Communists, that Germans were suffering and out of work.

The Jews as Scapegoats. Jews had lived in the lands now called Germany for over sixteen hundred years. They had come as traders following the Roman legions and had stayed and been joined by more Jews. Through the years, they had grown to a sizable community. About one hundred thousand Jews had served in the German army during World War I (and some twelve thousand were killed in the fighting). By the late 1920s more than half a million Jews lived in Germany, about a third of them in the capital city Berlin.

Throughout the Middle Ages the Jews had been victims of hatred in Germany, as they had in much of Christian Europe. They were often accused of being "Christ-killers" who had murdered Jesus. They were believed to practice black magic. They were accused of poisoning wells from which the Christians drew their water (especially during epidemics such as the Black Plague). Among the occupations open to Jews were small trades and moneylending (defined as a sinful occupation by the Catholic Church). Jews were therefore often accused of cheating Christians in business and in banking. Germany, along with other

European countries, had a long history of using the Jews as scapegoats.

The idea of a scapegoat comes, strangely enough, from an ancient Jewish practice. In Biblical times, when the sacrifice of animals was common, the Jews would select a goat from the flocks before the holy day of Yom Kippur (on which, it was said, God judged the sins of all people). The priests would announce that all the sins of the past year were placed on the head of the goat and the animal was turned loose into the wilderness. The people believed that this would ensure God's forgiveness, and their lives would be spared for another year.

But the idea of choosing a scapegoat came to have another meaning as well. A scapegoat is any person or group of people singled out to bear the blame for others.

Racism. Hitler used the Jews as scapegoats to bear the blame for all of Germany's problems. He counted on the fact that there had been many long years of religious prejudice against Jews in the minds of the German people; but he counted even more on a modern kind of anti-Semitism—racism. Hitler spread the idea that the Jews were a separate "race," a group with specific inherited qualities. Hitler's anti-Semitism was further based on the belief that these "inherited" Jewish qualities were wicked, ignoble, and inferior. These were among the ideas that he had set forth in his book *Mein Kampf*.

The idea of racism is that race determines human abilities and qualities, making some racial groups inferior and some superior. This idea was widespread in Hitler's time. What made racism so convincing in

Hitler's propaganda was the fact that the peoples of the world may indeed be divided into several races, each with its own physical characteristics.

But Hitler and others added cultural and psychological values to the idea of race. Hitler claimed that each race also had its own particular blood. He warned of the dangers of allowing these blood strains to be mixed. Hitler and some of the scientists of his day also claimed that a person's blood controlled his or her personality; one kind of blood would make a person criminal, or cruel, or unintelligent. Another kind of blood made a person noble and pure. And, according to Hitler, the highest type was the Aryan blood of the German race. But neither skin color nor race determines these qualities. There are good and bad people among all races. Blood has nothing to do with race either. All blood types exist in all races. And, most important, there are very few people whose race is "pure," that is, of unmixed descent.

The error becomes clear if we consider the case of the American Negro. Nothing seems plainer than the fact that he is a member of the black race. Yet one anthropologist estimates that probably less than one-fourth of the Negroes in America are of unmixed descent, and that in respect to alleged Negro physical traits, the average American Negro is as far from the pure Negroid type as he is from the average Caucasoid [white] type. In short, the average American Negro is as much a white man as he is a black man. . . .

Similar is the case of the Jew. It is convenient, but fallacious, to simplify the enor-

[27]

mously complex set of ethnic, religious, historical, and psychological influences that characterize this group with the label "race."

. . . Strictly speaking, all blood types are found in all races. [Gordon W. Allport, *The Nature of Prejudice*]

Using "Science" to Promote Racism. Despite the fact that most scientists disagreed about the idea of inferior and superior races, Hitler was able to use this idea as a basic part of Nazi propaganda. He gave the old, religion-based hatred of the Jews new respectability through the "science of racism." In fact, it became dangerous to disagree with the Nazis about racism. And it became clear that the road to success in Germany was to help Hitler prove that the Jews were inferior and untrustworthy—in short, the enemy.

Ignorant, prejudiced, and uneducated people were not the only ones to accept this theory. Many intelligent, educated Germans, too, went along with Hitler's ideas and believed his propaganda, or pretended to. Indeed, a number actively tried to prove Hitler correct and thus furthered their own careers in science, medicine, law, business, and the arts.

Textbooks used in schools and colleges were rewritten to teach what was called "German" mathematics, physics, and chemistry. These sciences were given a racial slant. For example, here is a problem taken from a basic arithmetic textbook approved by the Nazis: "The Jews are aliens in Germany. In 1933 there were 66,066,000 inhabitants of the German Reich, of whom 499,682 were Jews. What is the percentage of aliens?"

Even fairy tales were used as propaganda. Teachers were told to explain that Sleeping Beauty was really the German nation after World War I, and the prince who awakened her with a kiss was Adolf Hitler.

Did Hitler Believe What He Preached? Was Hitler himself convinced of the ideas he spread? Did he really believe that the Jews were a race, that they were inferior, that the blood of German Jews was different from the blood of German Aryans, that their blood would poison that of the Aryans? Or was he devious? Did he merely use these ideas and the ancient prejudice against Jews to help him in his rise to power?

Speaking to a close friend, Hitler had once said:

> I know perfectly well that in the scientific sense there is no such thing as race. As a politician I need an idea which enables the order which has hitherto existed on a historic basis to be abolished and an entirely new order enforced and given an intellectual basis. And for this purpose the idea of race serves me well. [Quoted in John Toland, *Adolf Hitler*]

In either case, it seems probable that by the end of his life, Hitler came to believe his own propaganda.

3
PUTTING ANTI-SEMITISM TO WORK

April 1, 1933: Hitler proclaimed a one-day boycott of all Jewish shops. German citizens were not to buy anything that day from Jews. On April 7 a law was passed forcing anyone not Aryan to retire from government work. All Jews in local, state, or federal offices lost their jobs. On April 21 Jews were forbidden to slaughter or prepare their meat according to Jewish law. On April 25 it was announced that fewer Jews would be admitted to German universities in order to make more room for non-Jewish Germans.

Jews began to flee the country. The government made them leave almost everything behind: their savings, their belongings, whatever they had. Many Jews refused to believe that things could get worse. They stayed in the hope that the anti-Semitic fever would soon cool. But it was more than a fever; it was growing into a madness.

The Nuremberg Laws. From 1933 to 1935 there was a short breathing space for the Jews. Almost two years passed while Hitler worked to make his government all-powerful, and no important anti-Jewish laws were passed. In August 1934 President von Hindenburg died, and Hitler declared himself chancellor and *Führer* of the German Reich and people. Hitler's growing power frightened the Jews, but the majority still stayed on. Germany was their home. Then in the fall of 1935 Hitler turned his attention once more to "the Jewish question."

On September 15, 1935, the Reichstag met in a special party congress in Nuremberg. For the Nazis it was a day of celebration. They had just passed the so-called Nuremberg Laws declaring that Jews were no longer German citizens—now Jews were "subjects." They were no longer allowed to marry German citizens or to hire German women under the age of forty-five as servants or household help.

In 1936 Jews lost the right to vote in elections. Stores, shops, lawyers' and doctors' offices, displayed signs saying, Jews Not Welcome. These signs were taken down when the Olympic Games came to Berlin in August. But they were put up again as soon as the flock of tourists from around the world had gone. Only token Jews were allowed to participate in the Games; and the Nazis were upset when a black American, Jesse Owens, won four championships in track events, breaking two world records and besting all the Aryans.

More Jews lost their jobs in the following years. In July 1938 the Jews were told they could no longer be brokers, office managers, tourist guides, or real estate agents. In September it was announced that Jewish doctors were no longer doctors but just "medical assistants."

Even Jewish names came under attack. Any street name that sounded Jewish was changed. Jews whose first names did not sound "Jewish" enough were made to add the name "Israel" or "Sarah" so that they would not be mistaken for Aryans. Jews had to carry special identification cards showing that they were Jewish; and in October 1938 all Jewish passports were stamped with a "J" for "*Jude*" (Jew).

Deportation. It had become very clear that the Nazis were trying to force Jews to leave Germany. But the Jews, like all other Germans, had suffered from the depression. Many were too poor to travel. And none of the countries surrounding Germany wished to allow those Jews who were poor to enter. Hitler turned the matter over to one of his lieutenants, Reinhard Heydrich. Heydrich's assignment was to find ways of forcing Jewish emigration.

Heydrich had to act quickly. Poland had just passed a law stating that any Pole living abroad for over five years would no longer be a Polish citizen. Heydrich knew that many of the poorest of Germany's Jews had originally come from Poland and were still Polish citizens. Somehow he had to send them back to Poland before the new law took effect on October 31, 1938.

Just before the deadline, Heydrich's men rounded up as many Polish Jews as could be found in Germany. Some fifteen thousand Jews were transported by train to a small town on the German-Polish border. Their money and belongings were taken from them, and they were pushed across the border into Poland.

The Polish border guards were so surprised that, at first, they began to fire their weapons at the approaching Jews. Finally, however, the roadblock at the border was lifted and the men, women, and children—most of whom had not eaten for two days—poured across the border.

One of these Jews was Zindel Grynszpan. From Poland he wrote to his son Herschel who was living in Paris. He told Herschel of the frightening trip to the border, the two days of near starvation, and the terror of walking into the Polish roadblock. Herschel, just seventeen years old, decided to take revenge on the Germans. On November 7 he went to the German embassy of Paris and asked to see the ambassador. Beneath his coat he carried a revolver with which to assassinate the ambassador. When he was told that the ambassador was away, he went out into the hall of the embassy, drew his pistol, and shot a minor German official, Ernst vom Rath. Vom Rath was taken to the hospital where he died two days later. Grynszpan was sent to a German concentration camp, and probably executed there. He was never again seen alive.

On the day that vom Rath died, November 9, 1938, the Nazi propaganda minister Goebbels called for demonstrations against the Jews of Germany for what the Jew Grynszpan had done in Paris. Rioting, he said, was not to be discouraged.

Kristallnacht. This "night of [broken] glass" took place in Berlin. For Jews it was the beginning of the end. Heydrich sent instructions to all local police officers not to interfere, and Nazi police actually took part in the "demonstrations" against the Jews. Synagogues were burned, stores were looted and destroyed, and apartments belonging to Jews were broken into and their owners' possessions smashed. Heydrich ordered the arrest of as many Jews, "especially rich ones," as the prisons could hold; from prison they were to be sent to the concentration camps.

On that night, November 9, and for the next two days, Jews were thrown out of moving trains and buses, beaten up, and humiliated. Those who tried to escape were often shot. In all, 191 synagogues were burned, 76 more were totally destroyed, cemetery chapels and community centers were torn down, thousands of businesses were ruined, large stores were destroyed, twenty thousand Jews were arrested, thirty-six Jews were killed, and thirty-six more seriously wounded.

Later, Dr. Benno Cohen of Berlin recalled:

I could not believe my eyes when I saw the Berlin synagogue burning. The fire brigade was there, but did not lift a finger. They were instructed to be on the spot only for the protection of the nearby Aryan houses. Jews were rushing into the burning building and saving the Holy Scrolls while the hilarious crowd all around jeered at them. [Testimony given at the Eichmann trial]

Much Jewish property had been insured by German insurance companies. And from all over Germany these companies began receiving claims. The rioting and destruction had lasted almost two full days, but it came to be known simply as Kristallnacht, literally, "Glass Night." For broken windows alone the claims came to six million marks. Hermann Goering, the Nazi in charge of Germany's economy, complained to Heydrich, "You should have killed two hundred Jews and done less property damage." But Goering ordered that the Jews pay for the damages!

New laws followed forbidding Jews to own businesses, or attend plays, movies, concerts, or exhibitions. Jewish children were expelled from public schools and special curfews were set up for Jews. Jews had to ride in the backs of buses or trains. Jews were not allowed out on the streets during Nazi holidays. Jews were forced to sell property, to hand over stocks, bonds, and jewelry to the government.

The War Begins. Meanwhile, Hitler had been making plans for war. He had put Germany back to work building up the army and navy, just as he had promised. In 1930 the last allied troops withdrew from the Rhineland. In 1936 Hitler remilitarized the Rhineland for Germany. No one opposed him. In 1938 he annexed Austria. In 1939 the Nazis took over Czechoslovakia. These countries were weak, and Hitler met with no resistance. In Czechoslovakia the German minority may have looked forward to better leadership under Hitler. And the rest of the world watched, hoping with each claim that Hitler would be satisfied. Hitler continued to speak of needing *Lebensraum,* "living space," for the Aryan race to expand. Since the time he had written *Mein Kampf,* Hitler had always thought of Russia as providing potential *Lebensraum.* But between Germany and Russia, there was Poland.

Hitler concentrated his army along the German-Polish border and made ready for a blitzkrieg, a "lightning war" on Poland. To make sure that the Russians would not interfere with his plans, Hitler made a treaty with the Russian Communist government. The two governments promised not to attack one another. This left Poland without protection.

On September 1, 1939, Hitler sent tanks and troops into Poland, as the German air force attacked from the sky. The Poles were defeated before they could get their outmoded forces into action. Within five days Poland had been conquered. On September 3 Britain and France declared war on Germany. World War II had begun.

4
WAR

France and Britain were hardly ready for war against Germany, but sides had already been taken. In the mid-1930s Germany and Italy had supported the Fascists in the Spanish Civil War. The two had forged an alliance, and they now became known as the Axis powers. France and Great Britain—later joined by Russia—came to be known as the Allied Powers.

Hitler wanted to fight against France and win, for he wanted revenge for Germany's defeat in World War I. And he very much wanted to conquer Russia and overthrow the Communists there. But he had no quarrel, he said, with Great Britain. Indeed, he admired the British for the empire which they had built, and for their mighty navy. He also realized how weak the Italians were. They were as much a burden as a help to him. Their Fascist government was a watered-down version of Nazism that Hitler thought was weak-kneed, and Hitler had little respect for the Italian dictator Benito Mussolini.

In the weeks following the conquest of Poland, Hitler was pleased to see that the Allies were taking no steps to attack his western borders. For one thing, much of the German equipment had been damaged in Poland. And for another, Hitler had placed most of his troops inside Poland. Germany might have been defeated had the Allies attacked from the west in those early weeks of the war before the German army could be re-equipped and transferred to the western front.

War in the North. Instead, it was Russia that next entered the fray. On November 30 the Russians attacked Germany's friend Finland and conquered it. This gave Hitler reason to be angry and frightened. More than ever he was determined to attack Russia; and more than ever he was afraid that his enemies would now join to come at him from the north, through Finland, Norway, and Denmark.

To keep this from happening, Hitler occupied Norway and Denmark. He forced the Danes to accept German "protection." Two months later, Norway succumbed. But both the Norwegians and the Danes proved to be thorns in his side throughout the entire war. Time and again small groups of Norwegians banded together to attack German installations and outposts in Norway; and the German navy was often engaged in battling Norwegian ships and sailors. Denmark refused to carry out Hitler's anti-Jewish programs and resisted every German attempt to deport the Danish Jews.

The West. With Norway and Denmark occupied, Hitler had to make a major decision. He wanted to attack Russia, but was afraid that France and Britain might finally take that moment to attack him from the west. He knew that his armies were not strong enough yet to fight in both the east and west. So at last he turned his forces westward. On May 10, 1940, the German armies entered Belgium and Holland to "protect" them from attack by the English and the French. Both countries fell to Germany within days.

It was part of a clever scheme. Just as Hitler had hoped, the Allied armies marched toward the Low Countries during those few days, while the main section of the German army began its march southward into France. It was only a matter of weeks before the French and British armies were trapped between the two parts of the German forces; their food lines to the south had been cut, and their backs were to the sea. Four tank divisions of the German army were closing in for the kill—and the British and French armies faced certain destruction.

But at that fateful moment Hitler sent orders to the front that stopped the tank divisions. The job of finishing off the Allied armies was given to the German air force, the *Luftwaffe*. The *Luftwaffe* had little success. The Royal Air Force gave protective cover as more than three hundred thousand British, French, and Belgian soldiers were rescued by sea at Dunkirk and taken across the English Channel to safety. Nevertheless, France—Germany's hated enemy—had been conquered.

Hitler's Hour of Victory. On June 21, 1940, France surrendered to Germany. Hitler was celebrated in Germany as the greatest military leader of modern times.

He had defeated the French, he had ousted the British, and he had conquered most of Europe.

For a while he thought of sending his troops into Britain. But between Europe and the British Isles there was the sea, and Britain still had the strongest navy in the world. So Hitler turned his eyes back to the east. Feasting on his victories, he was hungrier than ever to conquer Russia and to defeat the "Communist Jews."

Just as Hitler was about to attack and invade Russia, the Italians attacked Greece. As Hitler had feared, the Italian army was too weak to conquer the fiercely resisting Greeks. In the end, afraid that the British might come ashore in Greece to help the Greek army, Hitler sent twenty-nine divisions against Greece. It took only four weeks to conquer Greece, including the island of Crete; but it was a four-week delay that Hitler had not wanted.

Axis Politics. Hitler's alliances had not been helpful to him. Italy had proved next to useless. Japan, despite her pact with Hitler, refused to attack the Russians. Spain, which had also made a pact with Hitler, refused, for reasons that Hitler could not understand, to attack the fortress of Gibraltar. Taking Gibraltar would have made it possible to keep the British navy out of the Mediterranean, and might have shifted the balance of the war. But Francisco Franco, the dictator of Spain, had reasons for being a "nonbelligerent" ally of the Axis. For one thing, Spain was exhausted after its civil war. For another, although Hitler did not know it, Franco was partly Jewish. In the main, Germany had to go it alone in western Europe.

The Soviet Union. On June 22, 1941, three million German soldiers, more than 7,000 cannons, and 3,500 tanks crossed over into Russia. The Russian air force was quickly defeated by the *Luftwaffe*. Russian tank divisions were speedily overcome. But the Russian army continued to fight. The war in Russia dragged on; the precious months of summer turned to fall, then quickly to winter. It was October before the Germans saw Moscow in the distance. The weather was below zero in December, they still had not taken the capital city, and they were still in their summer uniforms. For Hitler it was all going too slowly. The blitzkrieg was turning into a suicide mission. And in the midst of it, on December 7, 1941, his allies the Japanese attacked Pearl Harbor, drawing the United States into the war. The Germans had had their hours of victory; now began the long slow days of defeat.

5
ISOLATION

As the German armies overran Europe, the Jews were trapped. Even while Hitler was directing the German military forces, he was leading the Nazi party in another war, the war against the Jews. In each country the Germans conquered the Nazi propaganda machine spread the lies of racism and anti-Semitism. In the conquered western countries laws were passed like those that had driven out the Jews of Germany or condemned them to poverty. As far as Hitler was concerned, France, Britain, and especially Russia, were merely political enemies. The Jews were far worse; they were "natural enemies" of the Germans.

To combat this enemy, Hitler used the tactics of modern anti-Semitism. But he also used tactics borrowed from the past: isolation and separation from the community.

Ghetto and Shtetl. In early medieval times, the Jews had chosen to live gathered in small groups around a synagogue. During the fourteenth century in Spain and Portugal they were compelled for the first time to live apart from non-Jews. Then in 1516, in Venice,

Italy, the Catholic Church ordered that walls be built around the Jewish quarter. Venice gave this compound the name *ghetto* which may come from *borghetto* ("little borough") or from the Italian word for a nearby iron foundry *gettare* ("to cast in metal"). At night the ghetto gates were sealed and guards were posted to make sure that the Jews would not come out until daybreak. In part, the Catholic Church wanted to protect the Jews from attack. Ignorant peasants believed not only that the Jews were guilty of having killed Jesus, but also that the Jews brought bad luck or practiced evil magic. So when things went wrong, or life became difficult, they would turn against the Jews. But in part the Church built the ghetto in order to separate the Jews from the Christians, and this isolation only served to make matters worse, for it heightened the superstitions of the peasants.

In a short time—and for like reasons—ghettos appeared throughout Europe. Jews were forced to wear badges on their clothing to show they were Jewish (this was another idea that Hitler would later borrow). By generally accepted practice, often written into Church law, Jews were not allowed to own land and were forbidden many kinds of work.

In eastern Europe, particularly in Poland and Lithuania, there were fewer ghettos. Instead, Jews lived in small private towns called shtetls. Shtetls were often protected by the government, and the government would sometimes use taxes collected from the Jews to support the local rabbi or even a town council. But the shtetl had much the same effect as the ghetto: it singled out the Jews and separated them from the non-Jewish world.

The purpose of the Church was to convert the Jews to Christianity. To achieve this, the Church did its utmost to make Jewish life uncomfortable. Jewish holy books were burned, and Jews were made to sit through long sermons promising hell to those who died Jewish. This was the great difference between the anti-Jewish behavior of the Church and the anti-Semitic behavior of the Nazis: the Church wished to destroy Judaism by converting the Jews, and Hitler wished to destroy the Jews themselves.

Jewish Values. In the ghetto and the shtetl a Jewish way of life grew up based on the teachings of the Hebrew Bible and the Talmud, a book of legend and law compiled by the rabbis of Palestine and Babylonia and completed in the sixth century A.D. In the Jewish world education was valued over riches. Outside, illiteracy and ignorance were common. Within the Jewish world schools were supported by the community; and most Jews—men and women—could read and write in as many as three languages.

At the center of the community the synagogue, the house of worship, was a gathering place for the Jews. There the rabbis and the teachers were the most respected citizens. Typically, Jewish time was spent in the study of holy books, in prayer, and in small trades. Each community had its own government, collected its own taxes, and had its own courts of law.

Partly because they were separated from their non-Jewish neighbors, the Jews learned to rely on one another. Then as today, every Jew was considered responsible for every other Jew. Everyone contributed to charity, even the poorest finding something to give. The family and family life were the core of the community. Within one's family one found entertainment and warmth, kindness and care.

The Jews learned in this way to survive attack after attack from non-Jews. After each assault life went on. Jewish merchants, bakers, tailors, and "fixers," as handymen were called, continued to work and trade with their non-Jewish neighbors. But they closed themselves off from friendships with non-Jews, and came to trust only in God and one another.

The Jews in the West. The way of life established in the shtetls of eastern Europe continued right down to the time of Hitler. But the ghettos in the west were torn down at the end of the eighteenth century when the armies of Napoleon Bonaparte swept across Europe. Bonaparte believed that the Jews would be loyal to him if he freed them from their walled towns, and he was correct. In time the Jews of western Europe told legends about the great Napoleon, and made him a part of their folklore.

When Napoleon was defeated, many of the things he had done were reversed, and a few ghettos were rebuilt. But for the most part, Jews were allowed to enter the mainstream of European life for the first time in hundreds of years. In fact, in Germany in the early years of the twentieth century, Jews were German citizens and fully equal with non-Jews. Some German Jews remarked that they were Germans first, Jews second.

Before Hitler came to power, German Jews had become lawyers, physicians, business people, writers, and professors. Although the Jews were only about 1 percent of the population, the majority of the leading German scientists were Jewish, a great number of them Nobel Prize winners. Two of Germany's greatest composers were Jewish—Gustav Mahler and Arnold Schönberg. And Germany had produced great Jewish writers; one, called the Shakespeare of the German language, was Heinrich Heine.

Many Jews stopped practicing Judaism and became "assimilated," or absorbed, into the general population. For these Jews it seemed that the ideals of Germany and those of Judaism were much the same. Judaism taught the equality of all human beings, and so did German law. Judaism taught love of justice, and so did Germany's greatest thinkers. Judaism believed in fairness and respect for others, and so did Germany's writers and philosophers. The position of Jews in Germany before Hitler was much like the position of American Jews today. Germany took pride in the achievements of her Jewish minority.

A New Time of Separation. But the mere fact that the Jews were outstanding in many fields made them noticeable. They were a choice target for Hitler's hatred. Hitler started out with a verbal campaign. Anti-Semitism became a dangerous and destructive social weapon.

> Using new means of communication, fascist groups have perfected the weapon of [anti-Semitism]. In its early stages, a fascist movement uses verbal violence as the precursor for the physical violence that will come later. [Carey McWilliams, *A Mask for Privilege*]

As his verbal propaganda campaign against the Jews took effect, Hitler turned to physical harassment. Separation became the first act in a large drama of destruction. The Jews found themselves trapped and held as in a vise. A Jewish Dutch girl, Anne Frank, was thirteen years old when she wrote in her diary:

> After May 1940 good times rapidly fled: first the war, then the capitulation [the surrender of Holland to the Nazis], followed by the arrival of the Germans, which is when the suffering of the Jews really began. Anti-Jewish decrees followed each other in quick succession. Jews must wear a yellow star, Jews must hand in their bicycles, Jews are banned from trains and are forbidden to drive, Jews are only allowed to do their shopping between three and five o'clock and then only in shops which bear the placard "Jewish shop." Jews must be indoors by eight o'clock and cannot even sit in their own gardens after that hour. Jews are forbidden to visit theaters, cinemas, and other places of entertainment. Jews may not take part in public sports. Swimming baths, tennis courts, hockey fields, and other sports grounds are all prohibited to them. Jews may not visit Christians. Jews must go to Jewish schools, and many more restrictions of a similar kind.
>
> So we could not do this and were forbidden to do that. [*Anne Frank: The Diary of a Young Girl*]

6
THE LADDER
OF PREJUDICE

By the fall of 1938 the first phase of Hitler's campaign against the Jews had been completed. The Jews were isolated and trapped. Anti-Semitism and Nazism had been linked together and identified as Germany's path to greatness and conquest. Scholars point out that such violent anti-Semitism did not come about by accident. Minor forms of prejudice have a way of growing into destructive forms.

In his book *The Nature of Prejudice*, Gordon W. Allport describes a kind of ladder of "negative actions" that spring from prejudice. It is interesting to compare how the ladder of prejudice worked in the past and how it works today. And it is possible to see parallels in history that help to explain or clarify what happened in Nazi Germany.

Speech. The first rung on the ladder of negative actions is *speech*. This often takes the form of talking or joking about a group as if all the members of that group were of one personality or had one set of features. One Holocaust historian, Raul Hilberg, states that "anti-Jewish racism had its beginning in the second half of the seventeenth century, when the 'Jewish caricature' first appeared in cartoons." The caricature, or stereotype, was usually an exaggerated drawing of a face with a long, hooked nose; heavy, dark eyebrows; a beard that came to a sinister point; and a protruding mole. This devilish-looking character was not supposed to look like a particular Jew, but like all Jews. The Nazis used this cartoon figure again and again in posters and artwork. Speaking, they referred to the Jews as "a disease," or as "lice." This was a generalization that harked back to the sixteenth century when Martin Luther, the church reformer, had spoken of the Jews as "a plague," and a "pestilence."

The technique of creating a stereotype is one which continues. It consists in giving an entire group a single, oversimplified image. For example:

> It is necessary for every White Racist to recognize the fact that the White Race does have enemies. We White racists must do that which is necessary to defeat the enemies of our Race. Certainly, the negro [black] is an enemy with his crime, his violence, and his high birthrate. Even in a more devastating way, the negro is a biological enemy and that is true of every negro who is able to breed. That is true because every drop of negro blood pollutes the White blood. The [child] of interbreeding between a White person and a negro, or part negro, is never White. . . .
>
> . . . That is why we must have a com-

plete separation of the races so that the White race can live. [J. B. Stoner, "The Philosophy of White Racism," *The Thunderbolt*, October 1973]

In this racist article blacks are stereotyped as being all alike: all are criminals, all are violent, and all have many children. Obviously this is untrue. Furthermore, the accusation that black blood is somehow able to "pollute" white blood is false, since it has been shown that all blood types occur in all races. Yet thousands of people around the world read publications like *The Thunderbolt* which are filled with such misinformation—and they believe them.

Avoidance. The second rung of the ladder of prejudice is *avoidance.* At this level people seek to avoid the group which has been stereotyped. Like speech, this seems harmless at the beginning. One has a right to choose one's friends, and choosing not to be friends with a particular group of people does not seem so awful. The trouble is, lack of contact and friendship with a group leads to ignorance about them. And the more ignorant we are, the more we begin to believe in the stereotype.

Discrimination. Avoidance leads to the third rung, *discrimination.* The unwanted group is now kept out of some neighborhoods, shopping areas, social clubs, gathering places, and public centers. The laws enacted against the Jews of Germany from 1933 to 1938 were discriminatory—they were meant to separate the Jews from the rest of the German population. Discrimination can be as simple a matter as

[53]

excluding Jews or blacks or Orientals from a fraternity or sorority or a social clique. Or it can be an attempt to cut an unwanted group off entirely, to isolate them.

After the Civil War in the United States, black slaves suddenly became free. To "keep them in their place," many of the southern states passed special laws to ensure that blacks would not be able to vote in elections. Blacks were not allowed to own weapons or buy liquor, to serve on juries or be witnesses in court.

> These black codes of 1865–66 in many ways resemble Hitler's laws against the Jews. . . . The white South wanted the Negro to stay, as a valuable worker . . . but . . . he must be prevented from getting "uppity," a word still common in the South. [Samuel Eliot Morison, *The Oxford History of the American People*]

Segregation—separation—of whites and blacks continued to be used as a method of social control. In 1870 a special school system was set up in Georgia, and blacks were forbidden by law to attend a school for whites. By the turn of the century South Carolina had special cars on each train set aside for blacks. In Oklahoma in 1935 a law was passed forbidding blacks and whites to boat or fish together. As late as 1944, in Virginia, separate waiting rooms were set up for blacks at airports. And throughout the South even into the early 1960s, stores and restaurants displayed signs reading, We Reserve the Right to Refuse Service to Anyone. The word "anyone" meant blacks.

Discrimination against blacks in the United States still exists. But the civil rights movement which grew in the 1950s and 1960s gave blacks a new sense of pride and helped them to fight for abolishment of discriminatory laws all across America. Of course, repeal of such laws does not mean that people will behave differently. To this day many blacks and whites have a hard time trusting one another; and in most cases, in the North as well as in the South, the two groups live in separate parts of cities and towns. This, too, is a proof of how powerful a weapon discrimination can be.

Physical Attack. When the Nazi party incited the riots against German Jews which came to be called *Kristallnacht,* they had reached the fourth level of negative action—*physical attack.* Physical attack may be a mob's expression of anger or resentment. It may take the form of gang warfare resulting from prejudice. (Many such gang wars broke out in New York City in the 1960s among whites, blacks, and Puerto Ricans.) Or it may take the form of defacing places of worship—for example painting the swastika (chosen by Hitler as the symbol of Nazi Germany) on the walls of synagogues or other Jewish buildings.

Such groups as the Ku Klux Klan and the neo-Nazis (new-Nazis) use forms of physical attack to frighten their victims. They burn crosses on the lawns of homes owned by black families in white neighborhoods, or they try to incite riots. From time to time, they have been accused of murdering Jews and blacks in cold blood. On the ladder of prejudice, the steps may be short between speaking against a group and attacking it physically.

[55]

Free Speech. Since prejudice begins on the level of speech, that would seem the best place to stop it. Yet in countries such as Great Britain, the United States, France, Canada, Mexico, Australia, and even West Germany today, free speech is guaranteed to all.

Because of this guarantee racists and neo-Nazis claim the right to preach whatever they believe, no matter how violent or undemocratic it is. Anarchists, who believe that all government should be abolished, claim the right to teach people how to revolt against government and destroy it. Communists claim the right to preach Communist takeover of government. Each group says that the basic right to freedom of speech allows it to teach and preach whatever it pleases—even revolution and the overthrow of democracy itself.

Should a nation then allow freedom of speech to everyone, at all times? Are there not times when limits must be placed on what should be said or taught? We already limit the freedom of speech where there is "clear and present danger" to public safety. But does freedom of speech or the rights of the individual include the right to spread hatred?

This problem faces us each time a racist or fascist group takes to the streets to hold a parade, or each time a public speech is made preaching racism. But who should decide what is allowable and what is destructive? And what measurement can we use to define the limits of free speech in a democracy?

It has been suggested that we draw a line between speech that is used as a weapon, and speech that is used to share ideas. But this difference is subtle and difficult to determine.

[56]

In a way, this seeming weakness of democracy is also one of its strengths. In a healthy democracy the exchange of ideas allows for many opinions to be shared. And all ideas must submit to open examination. Our continuing freedom depends, then, on continuing to examine our own ideas and those of others, and on standing up for what we believe to be right and just. Since voicing prejudice helps to create it, speaking out against prejudice may very well help to stop it.

Extermination—the Final Step. The last step on the ladder is *extermination*—lynching, massacre, attempting to kill members of the unwanted group. Between 1938 and 1945 the Nazis carried out a program of extermination against the Jews of Europe which they called "the Final Solution." We call it "the Holocaust." How the Holocaust was planned and carried out, and how the Holocaust continues to affect our everyday lives is the subject of the remaining chapters of this book.

7
THE GHETTOS 1939-1945

In September 1939 Reinhard Heydrich, the Nazi in charge of "the Jewish question" in Poland, sent out an order: all small-town and shtetl Jews in Poland were to be moved to the large cities where the Gestapo, the Nazi secret police, could "watch" them more efficiently. By 1941 most Polish Jews had been moved to the slums of Warsaw, Kovno, Krakow, Lublin, and other cities. Western Jews, including those of Germany, were moved eastward into Poland to join them. Walls were built to separate the Jews from the Polish people. The ghettos had been established.

The Warsaw Ghetto. Because the documents that survived the Warsaw ghetto are so complete, they provide a detailed picture of Jewish life in isolation. In Warsaw alone almost 450,000 Jews were squeezed into an area in which 145,000 had lived before. There were fifteen hundred buildings in the ghetto and about fourteen people lived in each apartment. There were no gardens or open spaces, so finding fresh air was nearly impossible.

With so many people in such a small space, disease spread and there were many epidemics. In 1941 a typhus epidemic struck. Doctors had little or no medicine, and 15,749 Jewish lives were lost.

But sickness was not the greatest threat to life. Hunger was. Cut off from the rest of the world, the Jews depended on the Nazis for food. The Nazis refused to give them meat, fish, fresh vegetables, or fruit. Instead, the Jews were given bread, potatoes, and fats to live on; and each person was limited to about eight hundred calories a day. (An adult male uses about two thousand calories a day just to maintain normal body weight.) People died by the dozens.

There were fifteen entrances to the Warsaw ghetto, each guarded by Polish and German soldiers who were told to shoot on sight any Jew who came too close. Only work gangs, closely watched by Gestapo men, were allowed to leave the ghetto.

Controlling the Ghetto. The Germans had no offices in the ghetto and seldom appeared there. For a while the Nazis amused themselves by conducting tours for German soldiers on leave, taking them into the Warsaw ghetto to show the Jews lying dead in the streets. But some soldiers did not find this amusing —in fact, they were so disturbed by what they saw that the Germans canceled these tours in 1942.

Control of the ghettos was put in the hands of Jewish "councils" or *Judenräte* (some handpicked by the Germans). They were told to obey German orders or be replaced. To enforce their decisions, the Nazis also set up a Jewish "police force." They tried to find Jews who would be a part of this force willingly, even recruiting some Jewish criminals. The Nazis gave these police forces uniforms, armed them with whips and clubs, and allowed them to terrorize other Jews. Many of these "policemen" were all too ready to comply, reasoning that the Nazis would spare them in the end. But in the end the policemen were sent to their deaths along with all the other Jews.

Finding Jews eager to cooperate was a favorite Nazi trick for controlling the ghetto. In one ghetto in particular they managed to find such a person among the top Jewish leadership. This was Chaim Rumkowski, head of the Lodz *Judenrat*. The Nazis saw in him a man who loved power, and so they gave him almost complete power. He was the ruler of the nearly 160,000 Jews in the Lodz ghetto, and he behaved as if he were their king.

Rumkowski often appeared in public surrounded by his admirers, wearing a white cape and hat. He raised taxes for the ghetto, coined money, and even had postage stamps printed with his picture on them. He reserved the right to arrest or pardon his "subjects." He told everyone that what he wanted was "peace in the ghetto," and that he hoped to save the lives of the Jews of Lodz. In 1944, when the last trainload of Jews was transported out of the Lodz ghetto, the Nazis stuffed Rumkowski aboard. They had no more use for him: he was just another Jew. But Rumkowski had served them well—there was never a rebellion in Lodz.

In general, the *Judenräte* tried to watch over the sanitation and health of the people in the ghetto, running its clinics and hospitals. They were also in charge of assigning people to work forces—both inside the ghetto and in factories outside the ghetto walls.

Everyone wanted to work, for those who did not

were soon rounded up by the Germans and sent away to concentration camps. People often tried to bribe members of the *Judenrat* to assign them work, and the members of some *Judenräte* soon discovered that assigning the "right" people to work could make them rich. In fact, bribery became a part of Jewish life in the ghetto.

Smugglers, for example, grew wealthy and powerful through bribery. They bribed SS men to ensure that shipments could be sent out of the ghetto and other shipments brought in. So small industries grew up in the ghetto which produced things to be sold outside. There was even one insurance company set up to insure shipments being made by smugglers. In Warsaw one smuggler became so wealthy that he gave parties for writers and artists and even ran his own ambulance service.

Children, too, became smugglers to help their families survive. Sometimes they slipped past the guards at the gates, sometimes through small openings in the ghetto walls, and sometimes through the sewers that connected the ghetto with the Polish city outside. Once out of the ghetto, the children begged and stole food and firewood to be taken back inside. Many families depended on their children to be clever smugglers.

Threats and Deception. In effect, the Nazis controlled the ghettos by a kind of blackmail. They said that if a certain command was not followed, or a certain number of Jews not turned over to them, thousands would be killed. In this way they slowly emptied the ghettos. They threatened the *Judenrat* to make them cooperate. If the *Judenrat* refused to turn over a certain number of Jews to be shipped out of the ghetto, then, the Nazis said, the whole ghetto would be wiped out.

Deception also played a large part in the Nazi strategy. For example, in Kovno in 1941 the Germans told the *Judenrat* that five hundred young scholars were needed outside the ghetto for a special task. They claimed that these scholars would be spared any hard labor. So the *Judenrat* drew up a list—young people even volunteered for this special duty. Five hundred Jewish scholars were taken away. They were never seen again.

Using the strategy of deception, the Nazis would say that those who had been taken from the ghettos were being "transported" to work in the east. Sometimes postcards came from those who had been transported; there would be one postcard saying they were well—and never another. There was never a return address.

The Jews began to realize that something unpleasant was happening to these people. They began to hear rumors that those transported were being sent to concentration camps and starved, or to death camps where they were gassed. But most of the Jews in the ghettos found these rumors too incredible to believe. What the Nazis were saying seemed more logical—that the Jews who were taken from the ghettos were being sent to hard labor camps.

By itself, that seemed harsh enough; and many began to resist when the Nazis came to transport them. Families struggled to stay together. Jews hid when they heard that the Nazis had entered the ghetto to conduct one of their regular roundups. The Nazis increased the pressure on the *Judenräte*. Any resistance, they said, would mean death for all.

Why Did the Jews Not Rebel? In the ghettos, too, death came quickly for thousands. Death by disease, death by exposure to the cold Polish winters, death by starvation. People suffered and died, but they did not often revolt. In his diary (July 1942) the famous Polish historian Emmanuel Ringelblum tried to understand why this was so.

> Why are they silent? Why do complete families die, father, mother, and children without a single protest? Why haven't we carried out the threats we made a year ago, the rebellions, the pillages, the threats that aroused the house committees and moved them to collect stores of food? [Emmanuel Ringelblum, *Notes from the Warsaw Ghetto*]

Time and again Ringelblum asked this question of people he met on the streets and friends he talked to in his home. Finally, he pieced together some answers.

First, was the fear of reprisals. The Jews knew that the answer to violence would be violence. If any rebelled, the Nazis would simply kill other Jews by the thousands. So, many submitted, hoping to save others from dying needlessly.

There were also those who did not wish to fight because they had found ways of "getting along" in

[64]

the ghetto. Some worked with smugglers or became smugglers themselves. People who were permitted to work wanted to go on working. Others had taken to peddling in the street, selling whatever they could for whatever profit they could make. The people who were "getting along" believed that fighting would only make things harder.

Many simple country people had been transported to the ghettos from the shtetls and small towns. For these people the city was bewildering, and the closed-in life was unbearable; they lost the will to live. Many of them had no homes; they slept and begged in the streets. Ringelblum reported:

> Recently I talked with one of these refugees, who had been starving for a long time. All he thinks about is food, particularly bread: wherever he goes, whatever he does, he dreams of bread; he stops in front of every bakery, in front of every window . . . nothing interests him any more. [Emmanuel Ringelblum, *Notes from the Warsaw Ghetto*]

Thoughts of rebellion had no meaning for people whose every waking moment was consumed by the search for food.

The Jewish police acted as another barrier to revolt. They were the only Jews allowed to carry weapons and they were more interested in having power over other Jews than in fighting the Nazis. They would not fight, and fear of them kept many another ghetto Jew from fighting.

The Struggle for Humanity. The Nazis were able to control the ghetto physically. Yet within the ghetto walls the Jews created a way of life based on Jewish values. They tried to feed their spirits, even as their bodies starved. Like Ringelblum, many continued to study and write. Reading became more popular than ever before, and the few books in the ghetto were read again and again, shared among all. *War and Peace* by Leo Tolstoi was a favorite book, for in it the tyrant Napoleon met his downfall. Unlike the Jews of western Europe who had been set free from the ghettos by Napoleon, the Jews of eastern Europe had no love for the French conquerer. Reading of Napoleon's fall, the Jews dreamed of a time when Hitler, too, would be defeated.

Schools in the ghetto had been forbidden by German decree, but teachers continued to work. They conducted classes for children and adults. Jews prepared for an imagined future by studying English. Diplomas were given, and being a good student was still a mark of pride.

Actors formed theater groups—amateur and professional—to entertain the ghetto. Those who could afford it went to the coffee houses at night to sip schnapps or watered-down coffee. Those who could not afford cafés gathered to tell jokes and stories. Though death was everywhere, young people still found the courage to marry and even to have children.

To Cooperate or Not to Cooperate. In many ghettos Jewish leaders refused to cooperate with the Nazis in deciding who would live and who would die. Dr. Adam Czerniakow of Warsaw finally drew the line at sending children to their deaths. Both Czerniakow and Dr. Rotfeld of Lvov, heads of their ghetto *Judenrat*, committed suicide rather than decide the fate of their people for the Nazis.

In Kovno the *Judenrat* called on the chief rabbi to ask what should be done according to Jewish law. The chief rabbi knew what Jewish law would normally say: no one should be given up no matter how many lives were threatened. But he saw, too, the people's terror; and so he ruled differently. Since this was a unique situation, he said, and the Jews were really all being held as hostages, the *Judenrat* should cooperate with the Nazis as long as they thought that by doing so some Jewish lives might be saved. But rabbis in other communities refused to allow any cooperation.

What seemed such a pressing problem at the time, proved of little importance in the end. Whether the *Judenrat* cooperated or not, the Nazis rounded up Jews and transported them to the concentration camps and death camps. All the threats and all the deceptions had been used to keep the Jews as peaceable and manageable as possible. From the outset, Nazi policy had been to send the Jews to their deaths.

Theresienstadt. In Czechoslovakia the Germans set up a special ghetto at Theresienstadt. Conditions there were better than in most of the ghettos and camps. To this "privileged" ghetto they sent well-known Jews, decorated war veterans, and old people. Of course, Jews who were transported out of this ghetto were sent to their deaths, but the Nazis kept life at Theresienstadt bearable for a very good reason: like all criminals, they wanted to hide the truth of what they were doing from the rest of the world.

[67]

When the International Red Cross came to inspect German ghettos or concentration camps, they were taken only to Theresienstadt. Nothing terrible seemed to be happening there. And that is what the Red Cross reported. As far as the outside world was concerned, Jews were not being mistreated.

8
CONCENTRATION AND DEATH

In the late nineteenth century, the British historian Lord Acton remarked, "Power tends to corrupt and absolute power corrupts absolutely." From Hitler himself down through all the Nazi leaders who were given power over the Jews, any personal sense of right and wrong was forsaken in favor of official government policy.

Hitler had chosen Heinrich Himmler to command the SS (which had originally been Hitler's personal bodyguard). Now the assignment to destroy the Jews was given to Himmler. For this task, Himmler used security police called the SD (*Sicherheitsdienst*), a branch of the SS. And Himmler placed Reinhard Heydrich directly in charge of the "Jewish question." Since the SD operated mainly within the borders of Hitler's Germany, Heydrich also worked with the Gestapo police to control the Jews in the lands that Germany had conquered.

It was Heydrich who discovered SS major Adolf Eichmann and brought Eichmann to Berlin. Eichmann had been tested in Austria. He had proved his abilities by setting up a remarkably efficient central office for Jewish emigration. Through the work of his office, Eichmann had "evacuated" 145,000 Austrian Jews from their homeland. ("Evacuation" was a term the Germans used for forced emigration.)

Eichmann was considered a kind of specialist in his task. Before the war, he had visited Palestine and studied Jewish religion and the Hebrew language. His report to the leaders of the SS concerning his travels in the Holy Land convinced them that Eichmann was an expert on the subject of Zionism. Heydrich and Himmler chose Eichmann to become the head of the "Jewish desk" in Berlin, and gave him extraordinary power—nearly absolute power—over the fate of the Jewish people in Germany and in all the conquered lands. From his small office in Berlin, Adolf Eichmann pulled the strings and made the decisions which cost nearly six million Jewish lives.

Executing Government Policy. Together, Eichmann and Heydrich planned the ghettos, intending them to be just stopping places for the Jews. They planned the transport of the Jews out of the ghettos, and they also set up a system in which large German industries could "rent" Jewish slaves from the Gestapo. Even the tactics of blackmail and deception used against the *Judenräte* and the Jewish populations in the ghettos were mapped out by Eichmann. He felt sure that these methods he had used so well in Austria could be used again in Poland and in Russia. As long as the official Nazi policy was to expel the Jews from German soil, Eichmann and Heydrich worked to do just that. They were no less efficient and no less devoted to their tasks when government policy turned murderous.

Scholars are still unsure as to the exact date of the Nazi decision to exterminate the Jews, but most agree that the decision had already been taken by January of 1942 when a meeting of high government officials was held in the Berlin suburb called Wannsee. Heydrich read a report prepared by Eichmann announcing the "Final Solution of the Jewish Problem." From the recollections of those who were present at this conference, and from records of the discussion which followed the report, it was clear that everyone present understood what this "Final Solution" was—the Jews were to be killed.

Definition of a Jew. A crucial question raised in the discussions at the Wannsee Conference was how exactly to define "Jew." According to Jewish religious law a Jew is any person born of a Jewish mother or any person who chooses to become a Jew by converting to the Jewish religion. This definition did not go far enough to satisfy the Nazis, for they were concerned with keeping Aryan blood "pure."

What about the child of a marriage between a Jewish male and an Aryan female? According to Jewish law the child would not be Jewish. But for the Nazis, the blood of such a child was impure. The Nazis said that such a child was a more dangerous enemy than the child of two Jewish parents. Aryan blood, they pointed out, made this child a born leader, while Jewish blood made the same child an enemy. The Nazis called these half-Jews *Mischlinge.*

[71]

At last a Nazi definition of a Jew was set down. A Jew was defined as anyone who had one or more Jewish grandparents. Many Christians thus came to be called Jews—even though they had been practicing Christianity for two generations.

The Einsatzgruppen. Even as the Wannsee Conference was taking place, Russian Jews were being murdered in special "actions." Groups of handpicked SS men called *Einsatzgruppen* followed the German army as it marched into Russian territory. They were the mobile "killing units" of the SS. In each town the *Einsatzgruppe* called on the local rabbi or Jewish town council, demanded a list of all Jews living there, and rounded up the Jewish community. Men, women, and children were marched or sent by train, truck, or bus to a nearby forest.

A ditch was dug to serve as a mass grave. The Jews were ordered to take off all their clothing, place it in neat piles, and wait. Small groups were then taken down into the pit. One German witness later recalled:

> The pit was already two-thirds full. I estimated that it held a thousand people. I looked for the man who did the shooting. He was an SS man who sat at the edge of the narrow end of the pit, his feet dangling into it. He had a tommy gun on his knees and was smoking a cigarette. The people—they were completely naked—went down some steps . . . to the place where the SS man directed them. They lay down in front

[72]

of the dead and wounded. Some caressed the living and spoke to them in a low voice. Then I heard a series of shots. [Testimony given at Nuremberg]

About eight hundred thousand Russian Jews were put to death by the *Einsatzgruppen*. In one of these SS "actions," some thirty-three thousand Jews were shot down in the Babi Yar ravine near Kiev. It was the largest single massacre of the war. Yet Heydrich and Eichmann both felt that the destruction was going too slowly. They began the search for a quicker way.

Death by Gas. It was Hitler himself who made the suggestion. As a soldier in World War I, Hitler had been caught in a gas attack. He still remembered the bitter, choking feeling of the gas and the fear that had gripped him. Gas was the perfect answer, he said.

In 1939 Hitler had begun a program of putting to death "imperfect Aryans," German children who were mentally ill or physically deformed. German doctors gave these children lethal injections in what was called euthanasia, or "mercy-killing." Now the doctors were told to experiment with gas. Several German chemical companies competed, each trying to make the most efficient gas for putting human beings to death quickly.

At last a gas was chosen to try at Auschwitz: hydrogen cyanide, called Zyklon B. It was made by a company which specialized in pesticides and poisons for rats and verminous insects such as lice. The company now went into the additional business of equipping gas chambers for the Nazi government.

Concentration Camps. The industry of death was now ready. All that remained was to bring the Jews to it. Throughout Poland and the rest of Europe, concentration camps were set up along the railroad lines. Jews were rounded up in all the ghettos and told that they were being shipped out to work in "the east." The program began slowly, but after Heydrich's death in May 1942, Eichmann proceeded more quickly. In Heydrich's honor, the project was named Operation Reinhard.

The concentration camps were more horrible than the ghettos had been. But the Jews were always told to have hope—it was Eichmann's promise to them, a lie repeated to each one of the millions who died.

Transports often arrived at the camps carrying Jews who had traveled for days without food or water. One train arrived at Auschwitz filled with people herded into cattlecars so tightly that there was only room to stand. Loudspeakers blared ordering people to get off the train and prepare to go to work. It would be good, the officers shouted, for the Jews to do something constructive with their lives. Men would labor; women would keep house or work with the men; children would go to school.

On the train, the dead and the living, many sick or wounded, stood closely packed together, refusing to move. German guards opened fire on them. Some Jews tried to run while others still huddled on the train. The guards shouted, "We know you want to die, but nothing will save you; you will have to go to work." Many of the Jews were convinced by these words. Surely there really was work, not death, in store. When they got off the train, forming a line, the

THE CONCENTRATION CAMPS

NORWAY

FINLAND

SWEDEN

North
Sea

Baltic Sea

Vaivara

Klooga
ESTONIA

LATVIA

LITHUANIA

USSR

Stutthof

Neuengamme

Ravensbrück

Bergen–Belsen

Sachsenhausen

Chelmno

Treblinka

Mittelbau Dora

Gross
Rosen

POLAND

Sobibor

Buchenwald

GERMANY

Auschwitz

Maidanek

FRANCE

Flossenberg

CZECHOSLOVAKIA

Plaszow

Belzec

Natzweiler

Dachau

Mauthausen

AUSTRIA

HUNGARY

RUMANIA

ITALY

Adriatic Sea

Jasenovac

Gospič

Sajmište

YUGOSLAVIA

0   100 miles

0   100 km

guards shot them down as well. Of that trainload, few survived even long enough to enter the camp. Hope and terror were arts the Nazis used skillfully to keep Jews under control until they could be destroyed.

Survival in the Camps. Inside the concentration camps there were Jewish police, prisoners known as "kapos." In return for special privileges, they forced other Jews to obey the Nazi orders. Here, however, there were also German guards (and sometimes Polish and Ukranian guards) always present, ready and willing to beat or shoot anyone who did not obey orders.

All the concentration camps operated in about the same way. At the entrance to the Auschwitz camp, for example, doctors sat behind a table. The prisoners were brought up to a doctor one by one. The doctor would raise his thumb and point to the right or to the left. To the left meant immediate death. For those who looked stronger, and were sent to the right, there was the concentration camp. Of course the Jews did not know what awaited them— they only knew that a selection was being made.

At Bergen-Belsen camp, tens of thousands of prisoners were crowded into barracks designed for a few thousand.

> The sanitary conditions were indescribable. There was one bathroom, always out of order, for a hut of four hundred people. . . . From time to time we would get what they called "soup." Then they almost cut off the food supply altogether. . . . Dead people lay

outside on the paths of the camp. . . .
Women fought in the gutter for scraps of
food garbage. [Testimony given at the Eichmann trial]

At roll call we had to stand about for hours
and hours in snow or rain, in heat or cold.
The standing alone exhausted us entirely.
. . . If anyone was late for roll call, the whole
camp had to stand on parade for many
hours, and he, the culprit, was beaten so
badly that he sometimes died of it. . . . We
had 2,200 patients in the hospital, and, in
addition, 15,000 sick women in camp, but
for a whole week we received only 300 as-
pirin tablets. [Testimony given at the Belsen trial]

Within their first few days, thousands died of hunger,
starvation, and disease. Some "ran into the wire,"
that is, they threw themselves against the electrified
fences of the camps. Still others died of cruelty—
beatings, torture, and worse. One who lived told of a
Nazi game at the Janowska camp:

A shooting competition was begun between
[two Nazi officers]. They would shoot out of
their windows at the people marching back
and forth loaded with stones, aiming at the
tip of a nose or a finger. The injured people
were "no good" any more and they would
finish them off with a shot. [Testimony
given at the Eichmann trial]

Diseases—particularly typhus—spread through the camps, but sick people pretended that they were still healthy enough to work. They knew that being sick meant death. Even escape meant death, for if anyone escaped, all the other prisoners in that group were immediately shot. The only resistance possible for most Jews was the effort simply to stay alive. To help them survive, the prisoners looked for ways of staying human, of not becoming animals. They began to live an inner life, one that the guards and the camp could not reach to destroy. For most it was a life of religion—it had been their mainstay on the outside, before the camps; and now it became their inner treasure. For others there was the chance to do some of the work they had done before—if they were doctors, they could help the sick as best they were able; scientists watched and memorized what they saw; historians and writers kept notes in their minds. Viktor Frankl, a psychiatrist, wrote of his efforts to help his fellow prisoners:

> The thought of suicide was entertained by nearly everyone, if only for a brief time. It was born of the hopelessness of the situation, the constant danger of death looming over us daily and hourly, and the closeness of the deaths suffered by many of the others.
> . . . I spoke of the many opportunities of giving life a meaning. I told my comrades . . . that human life, under any circumstances, never ceases to have a meaning. . . . They must not lose hope but should keep up their courage in the certainty that the hopelessness of our struggle did not de-

tract from its dignity and meaning. I said that someone looks down on each of us in difficult hours—a friend, a wife, somebody alive or dead, or a God—and he would not expect us to disappoint him. He would hope to find us suffering proudly. . . . [Viktor E. Frankl, *Man's Search for Meaning*]

Death. For those sent to the left at the first selection, the next stop was a death camp. Sometimes it was nearby. At Auschwitz, the death camp was called Birkenau and it was just on the other side of the electrified fence. Sometimes there was another ghastly train journey to be made from the concentration camp to one of the death camps. Sometimes the prisoners were gassed in trucks or in trains and never reached a death camp at all.

The prisoners sent to the death camps were divided. Men went to one side, while women had their hair shaved off. Men, women, and children were all told to strip. Naked, they were led to the "showers." As they passed through the doorway, they were given bars of soap to make them believe that there was still hope. Some believed it. Most smelled the stench of the camp and knew the truth. Mothers held their babies close to them. People began to pray; some sang. The SS men shoved them into the gas chambers, packing them in so closely they stood on each other's feet.

The doors and windows were tightly shut. At Birkenau, Zyklon B crystals were poured down perforated shafts. Some other camps used diesel engines to force carbon monoxide into the crowded room. The dead had no place to fall. They stood in death

[79]

as they had stood in life: families pressed together, holding hands; strangers with their arms around each other. Jewish workers had to separate the dead and put the corpses on conveyor belts.

At Birkenau the door over the gas chamber had these words written on it: This Is the Gate of the Lord into Which the Righteous Shall Enter. No doubt, this was Eichmann's sense of humor.

The bodies were placed in huge furnaces to be burned. The smell of death rose with the smoke and ashes. It pumped out of the chimneys and could be seen and smelled for miles around. From time to time Eichmann, even Himmler himself, came to make an inspection—to see that the gas was working properly, the machinery was in order, the furnaces were still operating. There was a special gate for the Nazi SS to enter at Auschwitz. Above it was written, Entrance to the Jewish State.

About 5,730,000 Jews passed through the doors of the death camps. At Auschwitz-Birkenau alone, some two million people were murdered.

9
PROFIT AND SLAVERY

From the beginning of the anti-Semitic campaign, the Nazis had found ways of making Germany richer at Jewish expense. When Jews were forbidden to practice as lawyers, doctors, and government employees, their practices went to non-Jews. German doctors and lawyers became busier and richer. Non-Jews took the office jobs left vacant in the government. When Jews were forbidden to sell to non-Jews, business became better in stores owned by non-Jews.

Aryanization. Goering, who was in charge of business and commerce in Hitler's government, announced to the world that "the Jews must disappear from the German economy." He meant to see that the property of the Jews, their belongings, their business and professional offices, would soon belong to non-Jews. By the end of the war nearly nine billion dollars of Jewish money, goods, and property fell to non-Jews through this "legalized" theft. There was even an official name for this transfer of wealth. It was called Aryanization.

In occupied territories such as Poland, Aryanization was carried out by the officers of the German army. One witness remembers:

> In the first three months of the occupation, the looting usually stopped short of the furniture. Later, however, the Nazis went . . . from house to house, and laid hands on whatever they could find. . . . In Cracow, on December 3, 1939, large military detachments surrounded the Jewish quarter at eleven o'clock at night. Guards were posted in front of the houses to prevent the inhabitants from leaving. The next morning at eight, all the houses were ransacked from top to bottom. . . . Officers did not hesitate to confiscate for their personal use such things as silk stockings, shoes, bedding, and even food. The search continued the next day and did not stop until half past two in the afternoon. [Quoted in *The Black Book of Polish Jewry*]

In eastern Europe where anti-Semitism was strong, most non-Jews felt that they deserved what they could steal from Jews because Jews were the "enemy." In western Europe (apart from Germany), where there was less anti-Semitism, the profits of stealing were enough reason for doing it. One Nazi chief in France reported:

> It is plainly almost impossible to cultivate in Frenchmen an anti-Jewish feeling based on ideological grounds [anti-Semitism], whereas the offer of economic advantages

could more easily create sympathy for the anti-Jewish struggle. [Quoted in Leon Poliakov, *Harvest of Hate*]

Jewish Books and Art. In March 1942 Hitler set up a special staff called the *Einsatzstab* to "collect" the most valuable pieces of Jewish art and literature. This happened as the Jews themselves were being transported to their deaths.

The Einsatzstab also collected Jewish Bibles, copies of the Talmud, prayer books, and books printed in Hebrew and Yiddish. Hitler wanted to be able to "prove" after the war was over that the Jews had been a true enemy. In the end nearly six million volumes were amassed in a mansion near Frankfurt to be studied by Nazi scholars who would try to convince the world how dangerous the Jews and their ideas had been.

But the *Einsatzstab* soon learned that works of art were even more valuable. These were given to Nazi leaders or placed in German museums. In a period of three years the Nazis collected more than twenty-one thousand works of art—paintings, drawings, miniatures, sculptures, medallions, and antiques among them. Works of art must not remain in Jewish possession, the *Einsatzstab* said, for the Jews might later sell them and use the money to fight against Germany. "Today's Rembrandt," they said, "is the financing of tomorrow's anti-German fight."

Jewish apartments were sometimes left fully furnished and given to Nazi officers as places to live. One officer, assigned a Jewish apartment, complained that the Jew who had been told to leave was packing his things and having them shipped to the Jewish quarter. This was stopped at once. "Luckily," the German officer wrote, "there still seem to be a few packing cases in the apartment. . . . Perhaps we can still 'swipe' something."

Slavery. It was not long before the Nazis found another way of profiting from the Jews. The SS, under Heinrich Himmler, began to use captive Jews as slaves. There was a new twist in the Nazi brand of slavery, however. Whereas in the past, slaves were valued for their labor, the Nazis saw no value in the Jews at all. Their idea of slavery was to work the slave to death. Himmler bragged that when he ran out of Jews, he would use Slavs or Poles as slaves.

The SS offered Jewish slaves for hire to large German factories and industries such as stone quarries, coal mines, glass works, textile factories, brick yards, and iron works. To keep the Jews working, the SS guard beat them or whipped them. Those Jews who fell down from exhaustion or refused to work were killed on the spot. The owners of the factories paid a small fee to the SS for each slave they used; and many new factories were built close to the concentration camps just to be near this cheap labor supply.

Forced labor took many forms. Jews were rounded up in Poland, for example, and made to clean the streets, dig ditches, build canals and fortifications, and even build the walls of the Jewish ghettos —the very walls that held them prisoners. Jewish slaves were used to dig out huge plots of earth that served as mass graves when the Jews of a town were machine-gunned to death. In the death camps Jewish slaves were forced to move the bodies of dead Jews from the gas chambers to the furnaces where the bodies were burned, and to remove the ashes of the victims and clean the furnaces.

One boy, sent to a coal mine near the Polish-German border, wrote:

> Why are we here? A hundred Jewish boys of fifteen, seventeen, and twenty, miserable and unhappy. Many of us have seen our own families killed. Apparently just to make us suffer. We are exposed to the jeers and mockery of the German brutes. On top of the blows: hunger. We were warned that if they found any bread on us beyond the ration, we would be shot. Fifteen days later there were only sixty-five of us left out of one hundred. [Private letter, quoted in Leon Poliakov, *Harvest of Hate*]

The Nazis' hatred of Jews was such that many Nazis wanted to make the Jews suffer, even more than they wanted to make money from Jewish labor. To these Nazis, slavery was better than killing the Jews immediately, for the slaves would first be profitable, then they would die, and they would also suffer cruelly.

"We Have Taken Everything They Owned." Even after Jews died, the Nazis found ways to make a few last profits from them. In May 1942, with the beginning of Operation Reinhard, the death camps began to work at top speed. Now gold fillings were taken from the teeth of Jewish corpses. Marriage rings and the last jewelry was taken from dead hands and necks. Shoes

[85]

and clothing were sorted for size and resold to non-Jews. (There were complaints when some customers found bullet holes in their newly bought coats and vests, or blood stains on the dresses they bought for their children, or yellow stars that had not been removed from the clothing before it was sold.)

Suitcases, thermos bottles, baby bottles, shawls, and blankets were collected from those entering concentration and death camps and resold. Eyeglasses and monocles were plucked from dead bodies. Artificial limbs were "recovered" from Jews who needed them no longer. Even women's hair that had been removed was used in the making of wigs or woven into "hair-cloth." The bones of some victims were ground into phosphate.

Even the graves of long-dead Jews were disturbed. The gates and funeral monuments of Jewish cemeteries were resold. Tombstones of Jews were used to pave the streets of German cities. Himmler said: "We have written a glorious page in our history. We have taken everything they owned."

10
ATTEMPTS TO ESCAPE AND PLANS FOR RESCUE

In the late 1930s, before the outbreak of the war, thousands of Jews fled Germany by car, by train, even on foot. Most went to nearby countries, remaining in Europe where the German armies later caught up with them. Other Jews traveled longer distances, setting out for North and South American countries or for Palestine. Some reached their destinations; others faced an unexpected ordeal.

The Boat People. The ship *St. Louis* set sail from Germany on May 13, 1939. Aboard were 930 German Jews bound for the United States. But people who wished to settle in the United States needed an immigration number. Immigration numbers were based on a person's country of origin, and each country of origin had a quota. Since so many Jews were coming from Germany, the German immigration quota had rapidly been filled. Over seven hundred Jews on the *St. Louis* had immigration numbers, but for most of them, there would be a waiting period of between three and three and one-half years before they would be permitted to enter the United States. Knowing this, they planned to wait in Cuba.

When the ship reached Havana harbor, however, the Jews found that the Cuban government had changed its mind—only thirty were allowed to land. Messages were sent to the United States, but the U.S. government refused to take any of the passengers in before their scheduled time. At last the *St. Louis* had to set sail again, bound for Germany!

Jewish leaders around the world went begging to government after government, even as the *St. Louis* sailed. No government would agree to accept all 930 Jews, but four countries—France, Great Britain, Belgium, and the Netherlands—finally agreed to divide the refugees among them. So it happened that many of the refugees found temporary safety in Europe, only to be captured again as the Nazi army overran France, Belgium, and the Netherlands at the start of the war.

Meanwhile, other boatloads of Jews were also turned away from port after port. Few places would accept them. Great Britain and Australia took in a few, but refused to open their borders to more. Switzerland even made it illegal for Jews to cross its borders (Switzerland had decided to remain neutral in the war, and wanted to give Germany no reason for invading). France, before it was conquered, refused to accept any large number of Jewish refugees, saying the country was already overcrowded with Jews. It seemed only logical that many Jews should turn toward Palestine (today's State of Israel), where a Jewish community was anxious to welcome them.

Toward the end of 1941, 769 Romanian Jews crowded aboard the small ship *Struma* and set out for Palestine. Palestine was then controlled by Great Britain. The Jews and Arabs living there were on very unfriendly terms (they would later go to war), and the British wanted to keep the Jewish population of Palestine from growing too rapidly. They decided to limit Jewish immigration. When the *Struma* neared Palestine, the British refused the ship permission to enter port.

The *Struma* next approached Istanbul in Turkey (another nation which was neutral). Here, the ship broke down. But the Turkish government would not allow the Jews to land without British permits for Palestine. Newspapers around the world reported the story of the Jews forced to live at sea, unable to find a place of refuge. But no government came forward to accept these Romanian refugees. Seventy-four days after the journey of the *Struma* began, the ship sank in the Bosporus a few miles from the Turkish shore of Istanbul. All but two of the passengers were drowned.

Rescue Plans. By August 1942 Hitler had destroyed as many as one and one-half million Jews. One American Jewish leader, Rabbi Stephen S. Wise of New York City, brought report after report to the State Department of the United States describing the Nazi plan for the "Final Solution" and giving evidence that the Jews were being sent to death camps and murdered. It was not until November that the State Department verified the reports and accepted the truth of Dr. Wise's statements. Even then no immediate action was taken. A declaration was issued by the Allies in December stating that the Nazis would be punished after the war for what they had done to the Jews.

But Stephen Wise wanted to save Jewish lives. In 1943 he worked out a secret plan for saving seventy thousand Jews. Money was to be placed in Swiss banks for the purpose of bribing Germans to save Jews. President Franklin D. Roosevelt of the United States gave his support to the plan, but the British Foreign Office wrote that they were "concerned with the difficulty of disposing of any considerable number of Jews should they be released from enemy territory." The plan failed.

Other plans were proposed, and failed as well. That same year, when the Nazis saw that the war was going against them, Eichmann agreed to "sell" thousands of Hungarian Jews in return for trucks, tea, coffee, and soap. The Allies refused to allow this exchange to take place, saying that these goods would help the Nazis in their war efforts and cause the war to last longer. One hundred thousand Hungarian Jews might have been "bought" from Eichmann and saved. Instead, most of them died.

In the view of the Allied governments, fighting the war was more important than negotiating for Jewish lives. Once Germany was defeated, they said, the world would be safe not only for the Jews, but for all peoples. It was a strong argument, but not convincing to the leaders of the Jewish world who realized that Hitler was determined to exterminate all the Jews within his power.

The Jewish scientist and statesman Chaim Weizmann of Great Britain tried to convince the Allies to accept a different kind of plan proposed by a Rabbi of Slovakia. He suggested that the Allies bomb the railroads carrying Jews to Auschwitz and other camps, and bomb the gas chambers and ovens in the death camps. But the British insisted that only military targets should be bombed—though in the end, the Allies were willing to bomb German cities, too.

Help From Organized Religion. For a long time the Jews hoped that the religious establishments of Islam, Buddhism, and Christianity might speak out against the slaughter of innocent human beings. Above all, the Jews hoped that the Pope, the most prominent Christian leader, would publicly declare his support for the victims and condemn the Nazi killing program. This the Pope was never willing to do. It may be that he was afraid of what might happen to the Catholics of Germany. Hitler could turn his death machine against Catholics as well as Jews. And what if Hitler won the war?

On the other hand, though the religious establishments did not speak out officially, many religious leaders did. Those inside the conquered territories—especially Catholics in France—risked their lives in doing so.

Out of their sense of what was right, religious individuals did even more. Many nunneries were opened to Jewish children who then could pose as Catholics and escape being rounded up by the Germans. Hundreds of Jewish children were saved in this way. After the war many of these children were returned to the Jewish community. Many were taken to Israel, and some were restored to family members who had survived.

The Protestant and Catholic clergy in Belgium did all they could to help Jews, especially Jewish children. One priest, Father André, arranged to hide many children. He even took it upon himself to continue their Jewish education rather than educating them as Christians.

Unsung Heroes. In addition to those who were rescued by the Catholic and Protestant clergy of Europe, many Jews were aided by hundreds of non-Jewish people who risked their lives to lend Jews a helping hand. In the Netherlands, Jews were hidden in the homes of neighbors who were not Jewish—in fact, so many were hidden in this way that the Nazis had to make house-to-house searches to find them.

When anti-Jewish laws were passed in France, one prefect of police, André Chaigneau, called a meeting of Jewish leaders to convey his personal apology for the laws and to promise that he would "not allow any arbitrary acts against the Jews" in his district. The French resistance forces made the smuggling of Jewish refugees across the Alps and the Pyrenees mountains a part of their regular activities. And the Nazis were once forced to arrest four hundred policemen in France who refused to round up and arrest Jews.

One Dutchman, Joop Westerweel, led group after group of Dutch Jewish youngsters on grueling marches to the foot of the Pyrenees where they crossed into Spain. In the summer of 1944, after many successful expeditions, he was captured by the Nazis. They tortured him and finally announced that he would be tried before a military court. He was allowed to write one last letter. He wrote to a doctor friend:

> I will not reveal any names [of those who helped me] . . . I am certain of this. I still feel strong. At night when there is a respite

[92]

from the torture, my wounds have a chance to heal. Mornings, when questioning resumes, I am rested and alert. I will remain silent. I am confident of this. . . . If we do not meet again, I hope that what we did together will remain a sacred memory for life. . . . [Quoted in Philip Friedman, *Their Brothers' Keepers*]

That summer Westerweel was executed by the Nazis. Along with many other brave non-Jews, whose names may never be known, he had risked his life and lost it.

There were even rare moments when a whole nation raised its voice to help. In the small country of Bulgaria, when the Nazis came to round up the Jews, people gathered in the streets to demonstrate, crying, "We want the Jews back!"

A Great Day of Rescue. More splendid still is the story of Denmark. The Germans occupied Denmark in 1940. For two years they tried to force Denmark to adopt anti-Jewish laws as other countries had done. The Danes would not cooperate. When a Nazi official spoke to King Christian X of Denmark about the "Jewish problem," Christian replied: "We have no Jewish problem in our country. The Jews are a part of the Danish nation." When the Nazis told King Christian that the Jews would be forced to wear yellow stars, the king replied, "If the Jews are forced to wear the yellow star, I and my whole family shall wear it as a badge of honor." In the end the Nazis stopped trying to convince the king to help them.

In August 1943 the Nazis issued an order for the Jews of Denmark to be deported and sent to the death camps. The Danes, learning that the Nazis would soon act, organized themselves into a nation of rescuers. Jews were hidden in their neighbors' houses, and smuggled in small groups to the fishing villages along the Danish coast. From there they were taken in fishing boats, pleasure craft, and sailboats across the channel to Sweden which had not fallen to the Nazis. Almost seven thousand Danish Jews—nearly all the Jewish population of Denmark—were saved in this rescue.

As if this were not enough, the Danes refused to profit from the absence of their Jewish neighbors. They protected Jewish property throughout the war; Jewish homes and apartments were sealed. After the war, when Jews returned to Denmark, they found their homes and apartments as they had left them, their businesses still waiting for them, their bank accounts still untouched.

A Jewish Rescue Team. The British finally agreed to help in a rescue effort in 1944. Thirty-two Palestinian Jews were parachuted behind enemy lines in the Balkans. One of these was Hannah Senesch who had a personal reason for wanting to go back into Hungary where she was born: her mother was still there. She and two others landed in Yugoslavia and secretly made contact with the Hungarian resistance fighters. Their troubles had just begun. When they reached Hungary and the Hungarians learned that the three were Jewish, they betrayed them to the Nazis. One, Joel Nussbacker, escaped by hiding in the French embassy in Budapest. The other two were captured, tortured, and finally put to death. Later, Hannah Senesch's diary and poetry she had written were found and published. Her name and the story of her heroism became a legend in Israel.

Joel Nussbacker, the Palestinian who escaped, managed to set up a small Jewish underground. Posing as German officers, he and his group saved several thousand Jewish lives. To smuggle Hungarian Jews out of the country, they forged hundreds of passports.

Nussbacker and the other Palestinians had wanted to do much more—to save all of Hungary's Jews. But it was not to be. Eight of the would-be rescuers were killed, some were captured and some escaped only after bearing Nazi torture.

The hard fact is that taken altogether, the rescue efforts of nations, of clergy, of individuals—both Jews and non-Jews—saved only a few thousand lives, while the Nazis managed to take six million.

11
JEWISH RESISTANCE

Why did so many Jews go to the camps with no struggle? Inside the world of the Holocaust the answer at first was hope. The Jews had hope that the war would soon be over, hope that rescue would come from the Allies, hope that their faith in God would protect them, and hope that life could go on.

In one labor camp there were fifteen thousand Jewish prisoners and only a few hundred guards. Asked why so many Jews did not attack their outnumbered guards, one survivor answered:

> . . . here we were still working. The Germans had told us they needed manpower. We thought: Who knows? Perhaps? . . . It was obvious that if anyone started the slightest open opposition, all these armed guards around us would immediately open fire. . . . It is a dreadful thing to stand opposite a machine gun and to watch a boy being hanged.

> . . . Then there was still the hope that this
> war was bound to end one day. Should we
> endanger all fifteen thousand men?
> . . . And once we had escaped, where could we
> go? [Testimony given at the Eichmann trial]

There came a time, however, when hope began to
fade. Word of German "actions" against Russian Jews
spread and the truth about the concentration and
death camps leaked out. Many Jews now began the
search for weapons and set out to resist the Germans
with force.

Nieswiez. On July 18, 1942, there was an armed revolt in the small Jewish ghetto of Nieswiez. The Jews
threw homemade sulphuric acid in the faces of the
German policemen. A machine gun had been stolen,
piece by piece, and when more German police came,
the Jews turned the gun on them. They set the ghetto
aflame, burning their own homes. In reprisal the Germans hunted down every last fighter; then they murdered all the other Jews who had lived in the ghetto.
This was the Nazi answer to resistance: whenever a revolt occurred in the ghettos, the Nazis would destroy
its entire Jewish population. In many cases the only
records we have of these revolts were kept by the
Nazis themselves—not a single Jew escaped to tell the
tale.

Partisans. Some Jews ran away to join underground
movements—resistance groups that existed in every
land controlled by the Germans. These groups were
made up mostly of young men and women. They
stole or bought guns and attacked the Germans when-

ever and wherever it was possible. In Poland they gathered in the forests and became "partisan" fighters, what today we might call guerrillas. They came out of hiding to strike at the Nazis, then fled to the forests where the German army could not easily follow them. Some Polish partisan groups allowed Jews to join them. Other groups were anti-Semitic, hating the Jews almost as much as the Nazis did. In some cases the Jews created their own partisan groups.

Every partisan's story is unique in some way, yet any one of their stories can illustrate what partisan life was like.

The Story of a Partisan. Sophia Yamaika was only seventeen, but she was determined to join the partisans, and she persisted in spite of one frustration after another. She escaped from the Warsaw ghetto in August 1942. First she made her way to a small Polish town where she hoped to make contact with a member of the resistance who would take her to a partisan group in the nearby forest. While she waited to meet the partisan, she hid in the only possible place—the Jewish ghetto. As it happened, the Germans came to round up Jews to be transported from the ghetto. Sophia was captured and put on a transport for the camp at Treblinka.

There were many sick and dying people aboard the train, and at one stop the Germans opened the doors to remove the bodies of those who had already died. Sophia slipped out and pretended to be among the dead until the train pulled away. Then she followed the railroad tracks back to town, still trying to find the Polish partisan who was supposed to be her contact.

Again she was unsuccessful. Her contact never appeared, and Sophia finally returned to Warsaw. She wandered the streets of the Christian city until at last she met a member of the Polish underground who gave her work on a secret anti-Nazi newspaper. In September, the Germans raided the newspaper and captured Sophia once more. She told them she was just a poor illiterate girl from the country who had been allowed to sweep the floors of the newspaper offices. The Germans put her in jail for a few months, but they never realized she was a Jew, and after a time they released her.

Still determined, Sophia made her way to the forest and finally made contact with the partisans. The group she joined was made up of both Christians and Jews, though the majority were Jews. Since she spoke perfect German she was assigned to spy work. Whatever she heard of German troop movements and plans she reported to her group in the forest. At last the partisans made a move, attacking the town of Gowarczow. They cut the telephone wires, destroyed the German headquarters, and burned the police station. They took lists of Nazi agents and local officials who had helped the Nazis. They were able to hold the town for five hours before retreating to the forest.

In February of 1943 the Germans sent three hundred men to attack and destroy the partisans around Gowarczow. The fifty partisans of Sophia's group had no choice but to retreat. Sophia and two others stayed behind to cover the retreat with machine-gun fire. Sophia died still firing at the German troops. It had been just six months since her escape from the Warsaw ghetto.

There were other small groups of partisans throughout the Polish countryside, but they were so few in number that they could do little damage to the vast war machine of Germany. Nevertheless, running away to the forests to join the partisans was the dream of many young men and women in the ghettos and concentration camps.

Resistance in the Camps. Those who could not, or would not, run away began to dream of revolt. The first problem was always how to get weapons. In Treblinka a Jew managed to get a duplicate key for the armory in which the Germans stored their guns and ammunition. A date and time were set to take the armory. A hand grenade thrown at one of the SS guards was the signal. Two hundred prisoners armed themselves. The gas chambers, the railroad station, and the guards' barracks were all set ablaze in minutes. The barbed wire fence was cut and torn away, and people fled toward the forests.

But the telephone wires had not been cut, and the Nazis were able to call for reinforcements. Hundreds of Jews were killed before they could reach the forests. A few escaped to tell about the revolt at Treblinka and word of this revolt led to revolts in other camps.

The Germans were ruthless in dealing with Jewish resistance. In one case, they caught a Jew who had planned a rebellion in the camp at Sobibor. They ordered him to reveal the names of others who had been plotting. When he refused, the Nazis brought out all the prisoners from his barracks. The Jew was forced to watch, as the Nazis cut off the head of each prisoner. Then they executed him in the same way.

[101]

Despite this there was a revolt at Sobibor. In the fighting three hundred Jews escaped from the camp. About one hundred managed to survive. The rest were caught and shot, but the camp was destroyed totally, never to be used again. The Nazis abandoned the Sobibor site.

Women resisted as bravely as men. At Auschwitz a Jewish woman named Mala became a symbol of courage and defiance. Mala stole an SS uniform and official documents which described the slaughter of the Jews at the camp. She managed to escape with the documents. A Polish soldier agreed to help her get out of Poland so that she could reveal to the world what the Nazis were doing. But Mala and the soldier were captured at the border and sent back to Auschwitz, where both were tortured. Mala was scheduled to be hanged in front of the entire camp. As the SS executioner—a woman—stepped close, Mala slapped her across the face. "I fall a heroine," she yelled, "and you will die as a dog." Mala's name became a legend at Auschwitz.

In 1944 there was a revolt in the women's camp at Auschwitz. Using dynamite that had been smuggled in stick by stick by girls who worked in the ammunition factory, the women blew up one of the furnaces. As usual the cost of revolt was high. All the women who had taken part in the revolt were captured, tortured, and finally hanged.

Rebellion in the Ghettos. In the ghettos it was usually young people—especially Zionists—who organized revolt. The Zionists were activists to begin with. They wanted to set up a Jewish state in Palestine. They were the ones who first believed the stories of those who had escaped from the concentration camps and death camps. Most Jews in the ghettos refused to believe these accounts, even when they heard them from eyewitnesses.

But the young people smuggled guns into the ghettos and prepared to fight. Young women acted as messengers, slipping out of one ghetto to carry news and smuggle weapons into another. And as time went on, no one could deny the truth of what was happening. Millions had already been killed. The underground resistance movements grew in ghettos like Krakow, Warsaw, Wilno, and Bialystok.

At Krakow, the fighters struck not in the ghetto itself, but in the streets of the town, surprising the SS men in places where they gathered to drink and talk. The Germans were taken unawares, and their losses were heavy. But as the fighting continued, most of the Jews were captured and shot.

Many of these younger people might have succeeded in escaping from the ghettos. But they were reluctant to desert their families or leave behind the old, the sick, and the children. They chose to stay and they died fighting.

The Warsaw Ghetto Uprising. The best-known Jewish revolt took place in the Warsaw ghetto. Plans were made long in advance. Guns and ammunition were smuggled in; grenades were collected; bottles were filled with gasoline and stoppered with cloth rags to make homemade bombs called "Molotov cocktails" that could be set aflame and thrown. Like grenades, they would shatter and explode.

[103]

In January 1943, with only seventy thousand Jews left in the Warsaw ghetto, a small revolt broke out. After it was put down, Himmler himself came to see what was happening. He decided that it was an ill omen: Jews were supposed to accept death quietly. He ordered that the ghetto be totally destroyed.

As they had done so often, the Nazis first sent the Gestapo to tell people in the ghetto not to despair and not to believe that Jews were being put to death. The Jews, they said, should go to the trains quietly, for they were being sent "to work."

This time no one was deceived. When German tanks rolled into the Warsaw ghetto on April 19, 1943, the Jewish fighters were ready for them. The Jews were led by a twenty-four-year-old, Mordecai Anilewicz, who commanded a small force of about a thousand fighters. All told, they had three machine guns, about eighty rifles, some hand grenades, some Molotov cocktails, and perhaps three hundred pistols and revolvers. They faced more than two thousand fully-armed German troops.

The Jewish force stopped the German tanks near the entrance to the ghetto. They blew up several tanks to block the streets, and the Germans were forced to retreat.

The Germans returned with more soldiers, and fighting grew heavier and heavier. The Jews were driven from the streets and the fight went on from house to house. In each house the Jews fought until they had no more ammunition. Then they hid in caves that had been dug beneath the buildings. As they retreated slowly, they continued to kill German soldiers. The German commander had to send for more troops.

A week passed and then two weeks, and the Germans still could not conquer the ghetto. On May 8 the Germans finally found the central command post of the Jewish fighters and set out to destroy it. Over one hundred fighters fell in that one apartment building. Many took their own lives so that they would not be killed by the Germans. Anilewicz himself died in the fight.

Still the battle continued. On May 22, Goebbels wrote: "The battle of the Warsaw ghetto goes on. The Jews are still resisting." By June the fight was over. The ghetto was burned to the ground. A few fighters escaped through the sewers. The Warsaw ghetto had been destroyed by the Germans.

Meeting Death. When resistance proved futile, many Jews met death calmly in the conviction that they were dying for a noble cause. Religious Jews said it was *al kiddush hashem,* "to glorify God." In the end, they believed, God would come to the aid of the Jewish people and the Germans would be defeated.

As the *Einsatzgruppen* stood ready to shoot Russian Jews in the forests, rabbis or community leaders would talk to their people or lead them in singing. Survivors later remembered some of these valorous speeches. One rabbi told his people:

We are suffering the worst fate of all Jewish generations. In a few minutes we will fall into this open grave, and nobody will even know where we are buried nor recite a prayer for us. And we yearn so much to live. . . . In this moment let us unite. . . . Let us face the

Germans with joy for glorifying the Lord's name. [Quoted in Eliezer Berkovitz, *With God in Hell*]

German documents captured after the war record that Jews went to the gas chambers with prayers on their lips or voices joined in song. Nazi officers were amazed by this behavior. They could not understand how a people they thought so inferior could die with such dignity.

The Last March. When at last the Germans realized that they were losing the war and that Russian troops were nearing the concentration camp at Auschwitz in Poland, an order was given for the prisoners to be marched back into Germany. It was a cold January day in 1945. Some 54,650 prisoners, all that remained of the millions that had been sent to Auschwitz, were taken out of the camp and marched westward. There was no food for them, and they were on the brink of exhaustion. Many fell along the roadsides. The SS men killed them where they fell.

> On some days there were as many as five hundred shootings. . . . We spent the nights in stables or just in the open. . . . Once they put us for the night into a very long underground excavation and locked the entrance. . . . We were suffocating but they did not open to our shouting and knocking. . . . The next day there were a thousand dead among us. [Quoted in Gideon Hausner, *Justice in Jerusalem*]

[106]

Those who survived the last march were placed in concentration camps inside Germany. There, the Allied troops found them—they were skeletons, starved and shrunken, with huge eyes staring out of swollen eyesockets. It was hard to believe they had once been ordinary human beings. Some were too weak to rise from the wooden shelves the Nazis had supplied as beds.

In the world of the Holocaust, survival itself had become the main form of resistance. As Gerda Klein, one of the survivors wrote, "It seemed almost a luxury to die, to go to sleep and never wake up again."

12
THE LAST ACT

On June 6, 1944, the Allied forces landed in France on the beaches of Normandy. By midnight the Germans had lost the battle there, and the Allies had a firm foothold in Europe. In July the Russian troops pushed forward toward Poland. Again the Germans were forced to retreat before them. By September American troops stood on German soil in the west. Hitler's world was slowly closing in around him.

In one last desperate attack Hitler sent his troops into the Ardennes forest of France, trying to separate the American and British armies. This was the Battle of the Bulge, the fiercest and bloodiest battle of the Second World War. It was over by January 16, 1945. No one had really won the battle. But Hitler's army had suffered heavy losses, from which the Germans never recovered.

Hitler's Death. Hitler went into hiding in a bunker designed and built for him beneath Berlin. In April most of the Nazi leaders left Berlin as it was being encircled by the Allied troops. Hitler refused to leave his bunker. Indeed, he never again left it alive. On April 30, broken by his defeats, Adolf Hitler shot himself. By his own orders, his body was taken just outside the bunker and burned. Hitler was dead, and with him Nazi Germany had died.

On the day before he died, Hitler wrote out a final statement to the German people. Nothing had changed for him, he said; he believed to the end all that he had repeated in speech after speech:

> It is not true that I or anybody else in Germany wanted war in 1939. It was wanted and provoked exclusively by those international statesmen who either were of Jewish origin or worked for Jewish interests. . . . Disloyalty and betrayal have undermined resistance throughout the war. It was therefore not granted to me to lead the people to victory. . . . Above all, I enjoin the leaders of the nation and those under them to uphold the racial laws to their full extent and to oppose mercilessly the universal poisoner of all peoples, International Jewry.

For Hitler the war had always been fought in these two ways: against the armies of other nations, and against the Jews everywhere within his reach. In his last hours he continued to urge the struggle against the Jews. The Holocaust was no accident of history; it was the plan of a racist who made himself an emperor.

But the murder of six million people could not be

carried out by one man alone. Thousands of Germans had taken part, and they had been helped by scores of other Europeans.

Whose Crime? After the war such people would say that they did not know what was happening in the camps, behind those barbed wire fences. Germans would claim that the slaughter had all been done in faraway places. How could they know about the *Einsatzgruppen* murdering thousands behind the Russian front? How could they know what was happening to the Jews of Austria, Poland, Czechoslovakia, Hungary, France, Belgium, Luxembourg, Italy, Romania, Greece, and Yugoslavia?

Even in these countries non-Jews grew silent about what they had seen and what they knew. Yet the truth was all around—in big city and in small town alike. During the war they had seen Jews being marched out of the ghettos to work in the factories, to clean the streets, to work in the mines and quarries. In many a home there was some piece of clothing, some painting or sculpture, some piece of furniture, some bedding or blanket that had come from a Jewish neighbor. What was happening could not be hidden from view. And when it was over, it could not be covered up.

Those who lived in the small towns near the death camps, those who owned or ran huge factories employing Jewish slave labor, those who had served as guards at the ghetto gates and in the concentration camps, and those who had been assigned to work in the *Einsatzgruppen* in "actions" against the Jews of Russia—all tried to forget what they knew.

The Record. At the very last the Nazis had tried to hide what they had done to the Jews. They made an effort to plow the camps under, to destroy the careful lists kept in the "books of the dead," and hastily to bury the thousands of corpses that lay piled high beside the camps. Eichmann worked feverishly to destroy the records that had been kept in his central office.

But the Allied troops came too quickly. Records were captured. Camps were still standing. The Nazi lists of the dead had not all been burned. Corpses still lay in the sunlight exposing the truth of what had been done. And there were still survivors to tell the story.

For nearly forty years scholars have been piecing this story together and still not everything about it is known. One thing, however, has become clear. Many of the problems and attitudes that gave rise to the Holocaust are still with us today.

13
ECHOES OF
THE HOLOCAUST

There was a widespread silence during the years of the Holocaust. It was made up both of words that were not spoken and actions that were not taken. Although the governments of the Allies knew what was happening in Europe, there was no great outcry—no mass demonstration in London or Toronto or New York or Chicago. The average person outside of Europe was hardly aware that millions of unarmed people were being condemned to death. Newspapers carried the stories of boatloads of refugees being turned away from Palestine or from the United States, from Cuba, or from Turkey, but people rarely asked what would happen to the refugees. They said little about it, thought little of it, and put no pressure on their governments to act.

Speaking Out. When the story of the Holocaust was revealed, it helped to break the habit of silence. More people made the decision to speak out. For the Jews it had been a costly lesson, and after the war Jews began to raise their voices. Jews joined the civil rights movement in the United States; Jewish women were at the forefront of the women's liberation movement; Jews took part in the movement to end the war in Vietnam; and Jews became more active in international affairs.

When it became known that the Soviet Union was oppressing three million Jews who were Soviet citizens—making many of them political prisoners and holding others who wished to leave—Jewish voices were raised all around the world. Lawyers traveled from the United States to join the defense of Jews accused of treason there. And non-Jews join the protests to governments and the demonstrations that continue to be held on behalf of the Russian Jews. Today people no longer feel comfortable standing idly by when events take place that seem to recall the Holocaust.

The New Boat People. A good example is the case of the boat people of the late 1970s. When the Communists took over Cambodia, Laos, and Vietnam, hundreds of refugees tried to escape by sea, just as the Jews had done thirty years before. They headed for Thailand, Malaysia, the Philippines, Indonesia, and China. Some traveled as far as Australia. As before, although their plight was reported in every major newspaper, it seemed as if no one would come to their rescue.

Malaysia turned back many boatloads of refugees, allowing only Cambodian Muslims to land. Hong Kong limited the number of refugees it would accept from Vietnam and Indochina. The Japanese allowed few refugees to settle permanently. One boatload made its way from Vietnam to Singapore where they were turned back, to Yemen on the southern coast of Arabia where they were sent away, to Japan—a journey of nearly 16,000 miles (26,000 km)!

Aboard one 20-foot (6.1-m) fishing boat were twenty-six refugees from Vietnam. Their leader kept a log in English in which he wrote about the journey:

> Aug. 22: . . . I saw a merchant ship . . . heading northeasterly. We tried to reach this ship with white flag and great hope to be saved. The ship changed course and increased speed. . . .

> Aug. 23: . . . At the worst time, the water pump broke down and water kept coming in the boat.
> In such a situation we saw a weak light. . . . Just as seeing heaven, we headed to the light. . . . Many of us were on the verge of fainting [from hunger and thirst].

> Aug. 24: At daybreak, we found out it was an oil-drilling station. We . . . approached her with white flag and SOS light signal. Nothing could have been more discouraging when some people signaled for us to go away and when we neared, the rope ladder was pulled up. [Quoted in R. Chartock and J. Spencer, eds., *The Holocaust Years*]

This time, however, the world did not wait to see what would happen. Rescue efforts were directed by the UN assisted by voluntary groups and government agencies. Refugees were resettled in the free nations of the world, "adopted" by church groups and charities. The new boat people were saved.

Detention Camps. Even in the free world we have seen government policies enacted that seem like echoes of the Holocaust. During World War II the United States government set up ten "relocation camps" to imprison 110,000 persons. Most of these people were U.S. citizens; all of them were of Japanese descent. At the time, of course, the United States was at war with Germany, Italy, and Japan, and the lessons of the Holocaust were still a thing of the future. But these detention camps seemed as arbitrary and unjust as any concentration camp to the people who were forced to live in them.

Only Japanese-Americans were held in camps during the war. There were never any concentration camps for Italians or Germans in the United States. Clearly, the Japanese suffered, as the Jews were suffering, from racism. Like the Jews, the Japanese who were to be removed from their homes and held in detention camps were identified by their blood. By an act of Congress in 1942 these people were defined as anyone with "one-sixteenth of Japanese blood." This was a shameful moment in the history of a country that prides itself on freedom, but it never became a Holocaust, and the camps never became places of starvation or death. In 1944 the United States Supreme Court declared the relocation camps unconstitutional.

Political prisoners in Russia today fare far worse in the Soviet labor camps of Siberia. Here, prisoners are treated as slaves. As in the concentration camps of

Nazi Germany, they are worked to exhaustion, underfed, and oppressed. It would seem that the concentration camp model has not disappeared from society. Nor has slavery disappeared. Despite international laws it continues to be practiced in parts of China and central Asia, in Africa, Latin America, and in some of the Arab countries.

Ransom. Today we are still confronted with the problem of how to respond to the practice—commonly used by the Nazis—of holding people for ransom. When Eichmann offered to "sell" Hungarian Jews in return for things the Nazis wanted, he was making a ransom demand. Terrorists often use this technique.

In September 1974, for one example among many, three Japanese terrorists invaded the French embassy at The Hague in the west Netherlands. After five days the French government agreed to the terrorists' demands. They released a Japanese terrorist who was being held in prison in France, flying him to Syria along with $300,000 in ransom money. In March 1980 a group of Pakistani terrorists hijacked a Pakistani airliner, successfully demanding the release of 54 political prisoners in Pakistan.

Other governments have refused to deal with terrorists. The State of Israel has set a policy never to give in to terrorist demands. In June 1976, an Air France airliner with about one hundred Israelis aboard was hijacked and landed at Entebbe airport in Uganda to be held for ransom. But the Israelis launched a surprise attack on the airport. All the terrorists were killed save one who was taken captive. One Israeli soldier was killed in the crossfire, and three of the Israeli passengers were also killed in the barrage of bullets. A greater number of people had been saved, however, and the Entebbe rescue showed that fighting back could be an effective way of dealing with terrorists.

The problem remains whether to give in to the demands of tyrants and terrorists in the hope of saving innocent lives (as many of the *Judenräte* did in the years of the Holocaust) or whether to strike back though lives may be lost. No nation is too big or too small to be faced with this issue. And that fact was brought home in 1979 when the staff of the American embassy in Iran was taken and held hostage for over a year by a revolutionary government led by a Muslim religious leader, the Ayatollah Ruhollah Khomeini.

Violence or Nonviolence. Perhaps one of the most difficult questions to arise out of a study of the Holocaust is the question of when to take up arms and fight. Jewish partisans, resistance fighters, and armed freedom fighters made a choice for violence—to strike back against the Germans although they knew they could not win. Many other Jews made a choice for nonviolence. They died believing their God would right the evil that was being done. The choice was not only whether or not to fight, but also how to fight.

Many people believe that nonviolence is the only real answer. Violence can only lead to total war, they say, and total war may mean the destruction of humankind. One of the first political leaders to prove the power of nonviolence was Mohandas Gandhi (1869–1948), an Indian statesman. Gandhi said that one must meet unfair treatment with "passive resistance," including civil disobedience and fasting. (At times he fasted for weeks in protest against unfair laws or unjust leaders.) As the attention of the world focused on his hunger strikes, Gandhi believed, his opponents would be forced to listen to him. Thus, Gandhi taught that suffering should never be inflicted upon the enemy, it should be used upon one's self.

Gandhi's nonviolent resistance was very successful. He first used it when the South African government passed anti-Indian laws. Within a few years the government gave in to Gandhi and agreed to lift these laws and end discrimination against Indians. Later Gandhi used his form of resistance in India to force the princes there to give up much of their power in favor of democracy. He was an important leader in India when the Second World War broke out.

Gandhi hated Nazism. Yet he also hated war. He believed that no war should be fought against Germany. He said that the world—including the Jews—should use nonviolent resistance against Hitler.

Gandhi's approach relied on the power of moral example. In nonviolent resistance, the victim sets the example, and sooner or later the persecutor is forced by the weight of public opinion to back down. (This idea was later used by some leaders of the civil rights movement in the United States, particularly by Dr. Martin Luther King, Jr.)

Yet in the ghettos and camps of the Holocaust, millions set an example of moral courage through nonviolent resistance—without any effect at all on Nazi policy or behavior. Moreover, Gandhi himself was killed by an assassin—as was Dr. King in the United States.

The difference may be one of moral education. People who are striving to do what is just may be better able to see the point of nonviolent resistance. But those who have little education, or have been raised in systems based on racism, may not have the ability to reason objectively. They may hear only what they wish to hear, and believe only what they wish to believe. And, educated or not, people do not always reason well when they are caught in desperate circumstances. As we have seen, the Germans after World War I were ready to accept any solution that promised to better their condition.

Like other issues which the Holocaust and its parallels have raised, the issue of how to resist injustice remains with us.

In a sense, all the questions raised by the Holocaust remain. Racism, prejudice, terrorism, slavery, violence or nonviolence, the proper limits to free speech—all these and more are issues that face us day by day.

14
WAR CRIMES TRIALS

In 1943 the Allies—including Russia, Great Britain, France, the United States, and representatives of the occupied countries—promised that when the war was over Nazi war criminals would be brought to trial. The trials were held in Nuremberg, Germany, beginning on November 20, 1945. They went on for 403 court sessions. Over one hundred thousand captured German documents were studied as the lawyers prepared for the trials. The record of the trials fills forty-two large volumes. The Nuremberg trials were the largest war crimes trials in history, but not the first.

Earlier War Crimes Trials. The first famous war crimes trial of modern times was that of Captain Henry Wirts, a Confederate officer who had been in charge of a prison camp at Andersonville, Georgia, in the United States. This camp, operated during the United States Civil War, had a reputation for starvation and cruelty that was not equaled until Hitler's time. Wirts was accused of the deaths of several thousand Yankee prisoners of war. He was tried by a military court, convicted, and hanged.

There were also war crimes trials following World War I. Most nations had agreed to certain "laws of warfare" drawn up in 1899 and in 1907. And the Geneva Conventions of 1864 and 1906 had laid down international laws regarding the conduct of war. The treaty that ended the First World War stated that the Germans had broken some of these laws and must stand trial for their crimes. A list of nearly 900 names was drawn up by the Allies, but only thirteen Germans were actually brought to trial, and six of them were set free by the German court that tried them.

Defining War Crimes. Preparing for the trials to follow World War II was a large job. Thousands of documents were placed before the Nuremberg court naming people who should be brought to trial. The international tribunal chose to bring to trial the top leadership of the Nazi party. Each occupying power was to conduct additional trials within its own zone. The tribunal's first job was to define "war crimes." The court declared that war crimes included "crimes against peace," including "aggressive warfare," and "crimes against humanity," such as

> . . . murder, ill-treatment or deportation to slave labor or for any other purpose, of civilian populations of or in occupied territory . . .

The top Nazis were clearly involved in such crimes, and so they were brought to trial. It was the first time in history that government leaders were tried by an international tribunal.

The Nuremberg Trial. A group of leading lawyers were hired by the court to defend the Nazi officers who could choose among them or request any other lawyer. These lawyers were faced by prosecuting attorneys from the Allied nations.

The prosecution tried to prove that the Nazis on trial had planned the war. They claimed that Nazis like Herman Goering, Joachim von Ribbentrop, Hans Frank (who had been in charge of mass murders in Poland), Julius Streicher (an early Nazi leader and anti-Semite), and Albert Speer, had planned to conquer the world if they could. As a minor part of its case, the prosecution presented witnesses and documents that told the story of the Holocaust. The defense lawyers could not say that the Holocaust had not happened, so they concentrated on other issues.

First they said the court had no legal authority. The defense claimed that the court was just a way of taking revenge; it was a "show" to justify executing the Nazis. But the judges of the court declared that "laws of war" and "laws of humanity" had existed before the war began. The Nazis were being tried fairly for laws they had broken.

The defense then said that the individual Nazis were only obeying the laws of the German nation. They were performing their duty. But the judges advanced a new idea—that some laws are "international moral laws." They pointed out that all people are aware of certain basic laws such as the law against murder, the law against enslavement, the law against extermination. Duty to these human laws comes before duty to any state or nation.

The defense now claimed that the Nazis on trial were "following orders." They were high-ranking military officers, and the first rule of all armies is that an order must be obeyed no matter what it is. On this issue the judges of the court declared that the higher a person is in military or governmental authority the greater his or her accountability.

The defense had one more argument. In Nazi Germany, they said, one man—Adolf Hitler—had given all the orders. Hitler was *der Führer*, the Leader, and to disobey Hitler's order meant death. This was called the *Führer-prinzip*, the leadership principle. In other words, the defense lawyers were saying, everyone in Germany had been forced either to follow Hitler's orders or be put to death. They were all innocent; only Hitler was guilty.

The tribunal did not accept this argument. They asked, how could any one man, even Hitler, have given every order? They had the document which proved, for example, that Goering had given the direct orders for the "Final Solution." And they further stated, as they had before, that it is in itself a crime to obey an order "which is clearly a crime against peace"—no matter who has given the order, or how great the pressure to obey.

When the verdicts were handed down, three men were set free. Although they had been part of the leadership, the court did not think they were guilty of crimes against humanity. Nineteen men were found guilty. Twelve were sentenced to hanging, including several who were pointed out as having had a hand in the murder of Jews: Goering, Streicher,

Frank, Alfred Rosenberg (who had been in charge of Jews in the eastern territories), and Arthur Seyss-Inquart (an Austrian in charge of Jews in the occupied Netherlands). The court had toiled to be fair. And the Nuremberg trials became a landmark in moral history, affirming that individuals are always to be considered responsible for their actions—in time of war as in time of peace.

Perhaps most important, the Nuremberg court had defined "crimes against humanity":

> . . . murder, extermination, enslavement, deportation, and other inhumane acts committed against any civilian population, before or during the war, or persecutions on political, racial, or religious grounds . . .

These are defined as crimes, whether committed by one individual or several.

The Aftermath of the Nuremberg Trials. The Nuremberg trials were long; they lasted nearly a year. Following them there were dozens of smaller trials of other Germans who had been important to the Nazis and who were accused of war crimes and crimes against humanity. Some had been in charge of concentration camps, death camps, or ghettos. There were trials of Nazi doctors who had used Jews as guinea pigs in unspeakable experiments. And there were trials of officers and leaders of the *Einsatzgruppen*.

Lawyers, judges, and statesmen knew that the trials were important—indeed, history-making—but most people in America and in Europe were busy returning to normal life. They soon lost interest in the trials and tried to put the war behind them. Even more disappointing, the Holocaust itself had played only a small part in the case against the Nazis, so it received little public attention.

Thus for many more years, the world was not really aware of the "Final Solution"—the murder of six million Jews, and the plan to kill all the Jews. To this day, there are many who do not know that Hitler proposed the same end for millions of non-Jews. He set out to destroy the Gypsy people entirely. He was responsible for the murder of Russian, Polish, and Slav civilians. His "Euthanasia" programs systematically took the lives of the old, the sick, the lame, the physically deformed, and the mentally handicapped. Yet even after Nuremberg, many people remained unaware of what the Nazis had done within the borders of Germany and the occupied lands. It was the trial of Adolf Eichmann in 1960 that finally captured public attention.

Adolf Eichmann. In the confusion following the war, some high-ranking Nazis escaped from Germany and Europe. Many of them went into hiding in the Americas, both North and South. After the State of Israel was established in 1948, a special section of its secret service set out to find these Nazis and bring them to justice. When Nazis were located in Germany or in other European countries, their names were brought to the attention of the local police and courts. Some of them were then brought to trial in Europe.

But in many places, especially in South American countries, the Nazis were welcomed. Bringing the name of an ex-Nazi to the attention of the government served no real purpose, since the government refused to arrest them, or put them on trial. Therefore, when the Israeli secret service located Adolf Eichmann, the Nazi who had overall responsibility for the "Final Solution," they did not go to the government of Argentina where he was found. Instead, they kidnapped Eichmann and took him to Israel.

On May 23, 1960, the prime minister of Israel, David Ben-Gurion, told the Israeli parliament that Eichmann had been captured, was in Israel, and would face trial under the Israeli "Law of Judging Nazi Criminals and Their Helpers." It seemed that the imagination of the world was captured along with Eichmann. Suddenly all eyes were on Jerusalem.

The Man in the Glass Booth. Eichmann's trial was world news. Because of it the whole story of the Holocaust and the "Final Solution" came at last to the attention of the people of the world. Eichmann chose his own lawyer, a German attorney who was paid by the Israeli government. For his own protection, Eichmann appeared in court inside a bulletproof glass booth. In front of television cameras, newspaper reporters, international observers, and world opinion, the story of the death camps and ghettos was finally told to the world, and the world was ready to hear it. Eichmann was found guilty, sentenced to die, and hanged. His ashes were scattered over the Mediterranean Sea outside Israeli waters.

15
GENOCIDE

The word *genocide* was coined in 1944 by Raphael Lemkin, a lawyer and a Polish Jew. It is a combination of a Greek word *genos* (meaning "race," "group," or "tribe") and a Latin ending *cide* (meaning "killing").

The Armenians. The Holocaust was not the first example of genocide in modern history. When some of Hitler's aides expressed concern that killing Polish civilians might rouse public opinion, he answered, "After all, who today speaks of the annihilation of the Armenians?"

Since early times the Armenians had lived in the shadow of Mount Ararat—the famous mountain on which, the Bible says, Noah's ark came to rest. The Armenians were the first nation to convert to Christianity; they have their own language, their own folkways, and their own church. But their homeland has often been a part of the Islamic empire, and they have often been persecuted by their Muslim rulers.

In 1915 the Turks, who ruled over the Armenians, declared that this small people was an "enemy" and must be destroyed. Just as the Nazis would do later, the Turks used war (in this case, World War I) as a pretext for accusing the Armenians of treason. They arrested many leading Armenians, put the men into slave labor groups, and embarked on a program of genocide. All those men who could not work were put to death. Gradually Armenian workers were also destroyed. Women were given a choice: they could leave their homes and their children to become the wives of Muslims, or they would be deported. Finally the Armenians that remained were driven into the desert where they died of hunger and exposure, or of whippings and wounds. Before the war there were about 1,800,000 Armenians in the Ottoman Empire (later called Turkey). After World War I it was estimated that two-thirds had been killed outright or driven into the desert. As a group the Armenians survived (two million lived in areas outside Turkey), but the slaughter by the Turks remains an example of attempted genocide in history. As Hitler said, few people remembered the slaughter, and not many had spoken out against it. It was not until after World War II that the problem of genocide was addressed by international law.

The UN Resolutions of 1946. After World War II, the Allies, led by Franklin D. Roosevelt and Winston Churchill, shared a dream that the nations of the world could come together to maintain international peace and security. Their creation was the United Nations, pledged in its charter to protect the rights of all individuals no matter what their sex, language, religion, or race.

From the first meeting of the General Assembly, the United Nations had to deal with the issues raised by the Holocaust. The UN set forth two resolutions based on the judgments reached by the court at Nuremberg. One declared that the nations of the world should bring to trial those accused of war crimes and crimes against humanity. The second declared genocide to be "a crime under international law." Thus the UN resolution of 1946 brought the word *genocide* into international law for the first time.

The Genocide Convention. Two years later the United Nations approved a "Genocide Convention," an international treaty that defined just what was meant by the word. Genocide was defined as acts committed with intent to destroy, in whole or in part, a national, ethnic, racial, or religious group. Genocide according to this treaty includes killing members of a group, causing serious bodily or mental harm to them, deliberately inflicting conditions of life on them that would bring about their physical destruction in whole or in part, imposing measures intended to prevent births within the group, or forcibly transferring the children of the group to another group. And the treaty makes it clear that these actions are considered crimes not only in times of war, but in times of peace as well.

However, since 1948, when the Genocide Convention was approved by the General Assembly, the world has seen or suspected other attempts at genocide. Those in danger are said to include blacks in southern Sudan, Kurds in Iraq, Nagas in India, Chinese in Indonesia, Native Indians in Paraguay, and Ibos in the Biafran War. But the United Nations was powerless to take action in any of these cases.

The Weakness of International Law. International law has not been very effective in these instances. The court has no power to enforce its decisions, and not all nations have adopted the treaty. Even after the Genocide Convention was approved by the UN General Assembly, it still remained for the individual members to adopt it. By 1951 enough members had approved it so that it officially took force. But many important nations, the United States included, have never approved it. Questions of national sovereignty are very delicate. The United States has refused to approve the treaty supposedly because it does not wish to give any foreign power the right to question the actions of the United States government. However, by not approving the treaty, the United States itself has weakened the force of international law.

Recently we discovered again just how weak international law is. When American hostages were taken captive in Iran in 1979, the case was brought before the World Court. The World Court ruled that the hostages should be returned and the arguments between Iran and the United States should be settled by negotiations between the two governments. Iran paid no attention at all to this ruling. And the court had no power to force Iran to submit to its ruling.

It would seem that international law alone cannot as yet offer real protection.

Revealing the Truth. How then can nations prevent events like the Holocaust? Information and education may be part of the answer. Understanding the past has a great deal to do with how we build the future.

For many years the Holocaust was not discussed in Germany. The Holocaust did not appear in German history textbooks. A whole generation of German youth was shocked when the Eichmann trial began, and later when television stations in Germany showed the film series called *Holocaust.* These young people could scarcely believe that Germans had done such things. Could it be that their own fathers and mothers had been a part of the Hitler Youth, or that their own grandfathers and grandmothers had taken part in the mass murder of the Jews?

But the more these young Germans looked at the evidence, the clearer it became to them that the calculated destruction of the Jews and the deliberate murder of six million other civilians was indeed ordered and carried out by the Nazis. The Holocaust is a fact of modern history—proof that extermination as public policy is possible, even in "civilized" nations, if their citizens do not speak out against it and act to prohibit it.

After the war a Protestant pastor, Martin Niemoeller, was one of several clergymen who signed a document declaring that the Christians of Germany shared guilt with the Nazis for what had happened to the Jewish people. Niemoeller had been one of the courageous few in Germany who spoke out when the Nazis tried to interfere with the independence of Christian churches. In 1945 he wrote:

In Germany, the Nazis first came for the Communists and I didn't speak up because I wasn't a Communist. Then they came for the Jews, and I did not speak up because I was not a Jew. Then they came for the trade unionists and I didn't speak up because I was not a trade unionist. Then they came for the Catholics and I was a Protestant so I didn't speak up. Then they came for me: by that time there was no one left to speak up. [Quoted in Philip Friedman, *Their Brothers' Keepers*]

Concealing the Truth. With no one to speak up about the truth, and with the press under control, the Nazis were able to use propaganda to cloak their activities. Nazis used euphemisms—special words like "Jewish problem," "Final Solution," "transports," and "work" to conceal programs of genocide and slavery. They encouraged people to believe that death camps were really work camps. They had orchestras waiting to greet the Jews who got off the trains at Auschwitz. The light music they played was intended to reassure the Jews and lull their suspicions even though death was planned for them. The Nazis referred to "showers" and gave the Jews bars of soap as they ushered them into the gas chambers. They used language and confusion to deceive their own people and their victims at one and the same time.

Perhaps no other time in history has taught us so much about the power of words to conceal facts. For a long time the Jews themselves believed what the Nazis said. They did not want to see that they were being led to slaughter. Softer words were easier to accept. German non-Jews also preferred to go along with what the Nazis told them. They did not consider that they were stealing from their neighbors, betraying people they knew, or allowing innocent people to die. Instead they accepted Nazi propaganda: the Jews were inferior, the Jews were enemies of Germany. And they preferred to believe that the Jews were being transported to the east "to work." Even those who knew the facts chose to close their eyes.

Afterward, when the war was over, many of these people went right on accepting the Nazi line. Even today there are Nazi groups in Germany still teaching Hitler's ideas. And they are at work in France, in the United States, in South America, and around the world, still spreading the same message. They are called neo-Nazis, but what they preach and what they are has not changed. And they are not alone. Many other organizations exist today that spread racist ideas using the same propaganda techniques the Nazis used.

The Need for Vigilance. The Holocaust was unique, and it is one of the best-documented tragedies in human history. Studying it is like passing a beam of light through a prism. Suddenly it becomes clear that the Final Solution was not one simple event, but a whole range of decisions, actions, and effects—a spectrum of the evil that human beings are capable of inflicting upon one another.

Today we see no immediate threat of another Holocaust. But familiar warning signs—the selection of a scapegoat, telling the Big Lie about that scapegoat, and directing the people's anger toward that scapegoat—still crop up in today's world. Only the vigilance of an informed public and the willingness of people to demand justice from their governments can guarantee that these symptoms will not come together once more to produce another tragedy for mankind. The Holocaust happened once; it could happen again.

SOURCES QUOTED

Allport, Gordon W. *The Nature of Prejudice.* Cambridge, Mass.:
    Addison-Wesley, 1954.
Anti-Defamation League of B'nai Brith. *Anatomy of Nazism.*
    New York: ADL, 1973.
Berkovits, Eliezer. *With God in Hell: Judaism in the Ghettos
    and Death Camps.* New York: Sanhedrin Press, 1979.
Bullock, Alan. *Hitler: A Study in Tyranny.* New York: Harper
    & Row, 1964.
Chartock, Roselle, and Spencer, Jack, eds. *The Holocaust Years:
    Society on Trial.* New York: Bantam Books, 1978.
Dawidowicz, Lucy S., ed. *A Holocaust Reader.* New York: Behr-
    man House, 1976.
Frank, Anne. *The Diary of a Young Girl.* New York: Pocket
    Books, 1952.
Frankl, Viktor E. *Man's Search for Meaning.* New York: Wash-
    ington Square Press, 1963.
Friedman, Philip. *Their Brothers' Keepers.* New York: Holo-
    caust Library, 1978.
Hausner, Gideon. *Justice in Jerusalem.* New York: Harper &
    Row, 1966.
Hitler, Adolf. *Mein Kampf.* New York: Hougton Mifflin, 1943.
Klein, Gerda Weissmann. *All But My Life.* New York: Hill
    and Wang, 1957.

[137]

McCuen, Gary E., ed. *The Racist Reader*. Anoka, Minn.: Greenhaven Press, 1974.

McWilliams, Carey. *A Mask for Privilege*. Boston: Little Brown & Co., 1947.

Morison, Samuel Eliot. *The Oxford History of the American People*. New York: Oxford University Press, 1965.

Poliakov, Leon. *Harvest of Hate*. New York: Holocaust Library, 1979.

Ringelblum, Emmanuel. *Notes From the Warsaw Ghetto*. New York: McGraw-Hill, 1958.

Smith, Bradley F. *Reaching Judgement at Nuremberg*. New York: New American Library, 1977.

Toland, John. *Adolf Hitler*. New York: Doubleday & Co., 1976.

Zisenwine, David W., ed. *Anti-Semitism in Europe: Sources of the Holocaust*. New York: Behrman House, 1976.

FOR FURTHER READING

Altshuler, David A. *Hitler's War Against the Jews*. New York: Behrman House, 1978.

Berri, Claude. *The Two of Us*. New York: William Morrow & Co., 1968.

Cowan, Lore. *Children of the Resistance*. Des Moines: Meredith Corp., 1968.

Forman, James D. *Nazism*. New York: Franklin Watts, 1978.

Meltzer, Milton. *Never to Forget: The Jews of the Holocaust*. New York: Harper & Row, 1976.

Procktor, Richard. *Nazi Germany*. New York: Holt, Rinehart & Winston, 1974.

Reiss, Johanna. *The Upstairs Room*. New York: Thomas Crowell, 1972.

Shirer, William. *The Rise and Fall of Adolf Hitler*. New York: Random House, 1961.

Stadtler, Bea. *The Holocaust: A History of Courage and Resistance*. New York: Behrman House, 1973.

Suhl, Yuri. *On the Other Side of the Gate*. New York: Franklin Watts, 1975.

INDEX

Battle of the Bulge, 109
Beerhall putsch, Munich, 13
Belgium: German conquest, 41; Jewish refugees, 88; attempts to rescue the Jews, 91–92
Belsen trial, 77
Ben-Gurion, David, 127
Bergen-Belsen camp, 76–77
Berkovitz, Eliezer, 106
Black Book of Polish Jewry, The, 82
"Black" caricature, 52–53
Blacks, discrimination against in U.S., 52–53, 54–55
Bulgaria, attempts to rescue the Jews, 93
Bullock, Alan, 22–23

Casualties of the Holocaust: Jewish, 1–4, 70, 73, 80, 89, 95, 110, 126; other, 4, 73, 126
Chaigneau, André, 92
"Chosen people," Jewish concept, 10
Christian X, king of Denmark, 93
Churchill, Winston, 130
Cohen, Benno, 35
Communist party, German, 19, 21–22
Compliance and resistance of Jews, 63–67, 78, 87–89, 97–107
Concentration camps, Nazi, 22, 68, 73–80, 85–86, 99, 101–102, 106–107, 111–112

Confiscation of Jewish property, 83–84
Control of ghettos, 60–68
Corruption in ghettos, 62
Cracow ghetto. *See* Krakow ghetto
Cuba, Jewish refugees, 88
Czechoslovakia, German annexation, 36
Czerniakow, Adam, 66

Dachau camp, 22
Dead bodies, stripping, 85–86
Death: by gassing, 73, 79–80; by lethal injection, 73; by shooting, 72–73
Death toll of the Holocaust, 1–4, 70, 73, 80, 89, 95, 110, 126
Decree suspending constitutional rights of German people, 19–20
Denmark: German occupation, 40; attempts to rescue the Jews, 93–94
Detention: by U.S. during World War II, 116; by USSR since World War II, 116–117. *See also* Concentration camps, Nazi
Discrimination as stage of prejudice, 53–55
Donne, John (*Devotions* XVII, 1623), 7
Dunkirk, 41

Economic gain from the Holocuast, 81–86

[142]

[144]

Roosevelt, Franklin D., 90, 130
Rosenberg, Alfred, 125
Rotfeld, Dr., head of Lvov *Judenrat*, 67
Royal Air Force (RAF), World War II, 41
Rumkowski, Chaim, 61

St. Louis, refugee ship, 87–88
Santayana, George, 5
Scapegoats, Jews as, 10, 25–26
Schönberg, Arnold, 49
Schutztaffel (SS, Blackshirts), 23, 69
Senesch, Hannah, 94–95
Seyss-Inquart, Arthur, 125
Shtetls, 45–48, 59
Slavery and forced labor; Nazi, 70, 84–85; since World War II, 116–117
Sobibor camp, 101–102
Socialist Party, German, 21–22
Spain, Axis partner in World War II, 39
Spanish Civil War, 39
Speer, Albert, 123
Stereotyping as stage of prejudice, 51–53
Stoner, J.B., 53
Streicher, Julius, 123, 124
Struma, refugee ship, 88–89
Sturmabteilung (SA, Brownshirts, Storm Troopers), 12, 17, 18–19, 21–22, 23
Sweden, attempts to rescue the Jews, 94

Switzerland, Jewish refugees, 88

Terrorism, 117–118
Theresianstadt ghetto, 67–68
Toland, John, 11, 29
Tolstoi, Leo, 66
Treaty of Versailles, 9
Treblinka camp, 99, 101
Turkey: Jewish refugees, 89; mass murder of Armenians, 130

Union of Soviet Socialist Republics (USSR): pact with Germany, 36–37; conquest of Poland, 40; German invasion, 43; massacre of Jews at Babi Yar, 72–73, 105–106; oppression since World War II, 114, 116–117
United Nations (UN): Resolutions of 1946, 130–131; Genocide Convention, 131–132
United States (U.S.): enters World War II, 43; Jewish refugees, 87–88; attempts to rescue the Jews, 89–90; Iran embassy seizure, 118, 132; World War II internment of Japanese, 116; Civil War crimes trials, 121–122

Values, traditional Jewish. *See* Jewish values, traditional